Merchant Prince

By Thomas McCarthy

Poetry

THE FIRST CONVENTION
THE SORROW GARDEN
THE NON-ALIGNED STORYTELLER
SEVEN WINTERS IN PARIS
THE LOST PROVINCE
MR DINEEN'S CAREFUL PARADE

Fiction

WITHOUT POWER
ASYA AND CHRISTINE

Memoir

GARDENS OF REMEMBRANCE

THOMAS McCARTHY

Merchant Prince

ANVIL PRESS POETRY

Published in 2005
by Anvil Press Poetry Ltd
Neptune House 70 Royal Hill London SE10 8RF
www.anvilpresspoetry.com

This book is published with financial assistance
from Arts Council England

Designed and set in Monotype Fournier by Anvil
Printed and bound in England
by Cromwell Press, Trowbridge, Wiltshire

ISBN 0 85646 375 2

One hundred and fifty *hors commerce* copies
of this book have been bound in cloth
ISBN 0 85646 382 5

A catalogue record for this book
is available from the British Library

In memory
of
John Bernstein

ACKNOWLEDGEMENTS

Acknowledgements are gratefully made to the editors of the following where many of these poems were first published:

Agenda, Poetry Ireland Review, The Irish Times, Irish University Review, The Record (New York), *The Shop, The Whoseday Book, The Clifden Anthology, Dancing with Kitty Stobling* (The Patrick Kavanagh Centenary: Lilliput Press, Dublin, 2004).

Readers in search of the originals of the Italian poets published here should look to the more authentic versions in the work of the nobility of that distant and perplexing kingdom, the Irish Language: Nuala Ní Dhómhnaill, Líam Ó Muirthile, Louis de Paor, Cathal Ó Searcaigh.

The illustrations are from various sources in Irish ballad-sheets and eighteenth-century prints in the Celtic Collection of the O'Shaughnessy-Frey Library at the University of St Thomas, St Paul, Minnesota. They were included in the author's *Six Years*, one of a series edited by Thomas Dillon Redshaw and printed by Paulette Myers-Rich at Traffic Street Press in 2004.

Contents

Blood

Nathaniel Murphy in His Sister's Bedroom, 1798   13
He Contemplates a Stolen *Bo*ʒʒ*etto* of Canova's
    Cupid and Psyche, 1811   14
He Remembers a Bottle of Léoville-Barton, 1807   16
He Thinks of the Meaning of Constant Happiness, 1807   17
He Considers His Wife, 1789   18
He Considers His Great Luck, 1812   19
He Remembers a Girl of the Callanans, 1829   20
In Illness, He Considers His Wife, 1827   21
He Watches His Wife Create a Silhouette Portrait, 1812   22
He Loses a Silver Ring of M. Billon, 1814   23
He Turns to His Wife, 1797   24
He Feels Moisture Falling, August 1st, 1802   26
He Spends Christmas at Clonakilty, 1809   27
He Buries His Father, 1809   28
He Goes Through His Father's Belongings, 1809   29
He Writes to His Estranged Sister, 1803   30
He Walks with His Son, 1799   31
He Mourns for His Nephew, Lt. Alan Mundy, 1814   32
At the Annual Grand Masquerade, 1826   33
He Meets His Future Sister-in-Law, Miss Teresette
    O'Neill, 1811   34
He Considers His Wife's Three Cats, 1793   36
He Recalls a Letter from Home, 1771   37
He Considers the Rev. Dill-Wallace, 1817   38
He at the Grave of Amadé Dill-Wallace, 1800   40
He Collects His Framed Etching of Cardinal
    Consalvi, 1823   42
He Prays to the Memory of Cardinal Ludovisi, 1769   43
He Contemplates His Failure, Rome, 1772   44
He Serves Mass at Advent, Rome, 1771   45

Trade

Nathaniel Murphy Disembarks at Passage, 1801   157
He Considers His New Eye-Glasses, 1800   158
He Recalls the *Jeanie*, America-Bound, 1775   159
At the Ordination of Father Layton, 1803   160
He Considers Four Young Nuns, 1789   161
He Considers Bishop John Bernstein, 1789   162
He Meets Eight Presbyterians Upon the Quays, 1829   163
He Addresses the Committee of Merchants, 1818   164
He Dines at the Nile Street Coffee-House, 1800   165
At East Ferry, 1801   166
He Remembers His First Meeting with James
     Barry, 1769   167
At the Castel S. Angelo in His Youth, 1770   169
He Remembers Cholera and Pine Trees
     at Naples, 1772   170
At the Adelphi, Thinking of James Barry, 1788   171
He Remembers the Val di Comino, 1770   173
He Recalls James Barry R.A., 1812   174
He Reconsiders Mr Barry's Neglected Gifts, 1830   175
His Tragic Sense of Life, 1831   176
He is Painted by Mr Daniel Maclise, 1830   177
He Reads a Poem of Dr Hickey's from Lisbon, 1831   178
He Buys a Copy of *Childe Harold*, 1814   180
At Mr O'Ferrell's New Villa, 1826   181
He Hears Memory and Praise of Bishop
     Clayton, 1797   183
He Learns of the Death of J.J. Callanan, 1829   184
He Contemplates the Autumn of 1814   186
He Witnesses Another Hanging, 1813   187
He Meets Lt. Hennessy, Cork Militia, 1799   188
He Looks Upon Another Dead Child, 1803   189
He Witnesses a Military Execution, 1804   190

He Considers the Misfortunes of Dublin, 1793   191
He Comes Upon the Cork Militia, 1798   192
He Purchases a Street Ballad, 1789   193
He Walks the Marsh, 1824   194
He Loses a Silver Buckle, 1797   185
His Tattered Copy of *The Mineral Waters*
    of Ireland, 1794   196
He Sees a Warehouse Burning, August, 1798   197
He is Overwhelmed by Edinburgh in Old Age, 1831   198
He Encounters the Poor of Cork Harbour, 1829   199

Blood

Nathaniel Murphy in His Sister's Bedroom, 1798

When my sister ran away with Polyphemus Shea—
A clerk from the quayside Custom House
Who promised her a life of Art in Boston—
She abandoned her cherrywood escritoire in the cave
Of her bedroom. My father's gift it was,
Made by the cabinet-maker O'Connell.

Like a buckle-thief
In Paul Street
I have removed the silver plate
With her names: *Letitia Louise*.

My only sister, so dear to me—
As far from her native Irish Kingdom
As Mr Singleton Copley is
From the quays of Jacobin New England.

He Contemplates a Stolen *Bozzetto*
of Canova's *Cupid and Psyche*, 1811

I place my hands on this abstract clay,
A reluctant *bozzetto*
That I bought for you, Miss Callanan,
On a rainswept Gironde quay.

Who knows which officer of the Empire,
Which prelate of the Gallican Church,
Placed it upon a north-bound cart,
Ill and creaking like a kidnapped Pope.

Out of Città Vecchia, once,
The frigates of Europe fled with art.
I found it on sale near the Barton wines:
All business done, thinking of you.

My hands grew warm upon its abstract
And unfinished form.
I thought of your love, the warmth
Of sacraments, harmonies pressed open

By the art of our marriage:
Fifteen years this piece has graced our room
As certain-faithful as the morning sun
Rises behind our Montenotte wall.

I prefer its unfinished clay
To Canova's more perfect *Cupid and Psyche*.
There is, beloved Miss Callanan,
A contrapuntal harmony we recognize

As vulnerable as unfinished art—
I would not claim a perfect unity
For us, mere humans that we are,
Any more than kingdoms far apart:

Slim, adolescent limbs that promise much
In an unbroken marital sense
Are like idyllic, mystical unions embodied here,
Born of Italian clay, Canova-like, yet deeper.

He Remembers a Bottle of Léoville-Barton, 1807

There, the hot summer before I met you:
Immortal France was set before me, Miss Callanan.
Two of the best-loved aristocrats of St Julien,
Ronald Barton, Anthony Barton, two of the few
Who survived exile and revolution,
Fermanagh, Tipperary, the port of Bordeaux.
Both sat beside me at the congested Puillac *quai*.
Wines of St Julien became a lover's profusion.

Miss Callanan, here is a glass in your beloved hand.
Léoville, Poyferré, Las-Cases, names that have the colour
Of your newest skirt, or of the Jacobin clematis,
With tannin as deep as love itself. As deep as France
In our Irish veins: this you understand.

Love changes a man's character the way a great wine does,
But retains its own memory like a concordat of quays.

He Thinks of the Meaning
of Constant Happiness, 1807

You wait for me against the marble portico
Of The Cork Library.
Rain sparks about your parasol
The way flints ignite what is tinder-dry.
Heavy drops become grey flares
As if the assembled ships
Of East Ferry and Lough Mahon
Had heaved-to to celebrate you.
You stand in their grey regatta of rain

And turn to greet me with an owner's love,
The way ships have an owner, or valuables
Held in secure bond. You walk,
Miss Callanan, with the tall grace of your mother,
A tall raven of the Corbetts.

I think of the love between us, a persistent
Bird of fair weather that survives rain—
And all the other elements;
Even time that takes the bond of books away,
Time that shields us like a parasol.

He Considers His Wife, 1789

For me your coolness is flamboyant as Scarlatti.
The sinfonia is yours
When you pass before me in a sedan chair
On your way to Bolster's Bookshop.
Your voice, when it reaches me
Across the two hundred and eighty four traventine
Columns, is piano and forte, loud and soft:
Loud only with the effects of *Orfeo*,
Soft only with the depths of a loved word.

On the first day I followed your voice
Over the North Gate Bridge.
That noon I became more than a city merchant.
The hours waved in welcome to your madrigal.

I was made whole by your indifferent glide past.
Such gestures and strength! In you the Baroque
Of our city became bearable.

Dogs may bark at the lepers in Tivoli Wood,
Labourers shout from Mr Beale's garden;
But you slot into the sedan of each tasselled year.
Your birthday, Miss Callanan—
The years Horatian and good.

He Considers His Great Luck, 1812

(for Catherine)

The moment that is lost is hardly ever found again,
As this minute, as the century.
Your love when I found it was there a brief day
For the asking, but you and your Sisters
And the Ursulines home from Havre
Might easily have snatched you away again—

Most utterly loved woman, most Callanan-like.

Out of this harbour the unlicensed ships sail.
The wind catches them, the fingers of heaven.
Even the most skilled Master can only protect
But not bring home cinnamon, nor profit.

One moment in my life I did sail beyond Roche's Point
So that you might catch my sail, my merchant eye.

I have traded off your love all my life—
The way a Bishop, the way a good Prince ventures forth.

He Remembers a Girl of the Callanans, 1829

That time,
          Before gas-lamps in Clonakilty,
You lit the first candle
          In the house
To read a sheet of luminous German music.
          Its damp light
Licked your left ear while you sat still.
Clear notes from your mother's violin
          Fell in pear shapes between you.

This night, now, the wind gets up.
          Schooners are restless in Lough Mahon.
I think of the exotic sadness in you then
          That so compelled
An unhappy young merchant to fall in love:
          Candle-light that licked you
I was envious of.
          The late September night
That needed to fold itself into you
          I violently
Envied. The dark of love unanswered I suddenly understood.

In Illness, He Considers His Wife, 1827

When I consider all your hoarded gifts,
Discretion in times of trouble, long passion
And its conspicuous impressions, quick tact
When provoked by idiots, I must grapple
For the words that name you properly.

You could have written the *Letters*
                    Of Madame de Sevigné,
Or the ambitious novels of Miss Austen
Or Mrs Barbauld's *Hymns and Early Lessons*.
When I think of the force and promptitude
Of your sympathies, your devout attachments,
I am as grief-stricken as Madame de Staël.

To have become a merchant's wife is not enough,
My beloved. I can see the piece-meal irritations
Of Montenotte life. Old Mr Jeffrey thinks
Your proper and natural business is to serve—
                    I disagree most violently.

I can tell from your sister's cryptic notes,
The long Latin phrases you teach our daughter,
The darkness of your eyes in Mr Barry's painting,
That you still have things most dangerous to tell.

Beloved, though you may never be famous in Edinburgh
Yet cast away doubt; labour long; publish well.

He Watches His Wife Create
a Silhouette Portrait, 1812

Sunday afternoon light falls on the still pools
Of rejected paper. A flotilla
Of shapes assembles about her feet:

All concentration in her perfect fingers,
My own beloved Miss Callanan
Cuts from memory the coal-black card.
I watch the anchor-chains of paper unfold
To lie upon the surface of her shoes.

It is a convict's head, one bound for Van Diemen's Land,
That we saw for less than three minutes
When our carriage turned into the Lower Quay.

Voilà! The image becomes itself
When she raises her arms to the window:
One convict that dares not leave
The native earth
Of her loose-bound silhouette-book.

He Loses a Silver Ring of M. Billon, 1814

It was something I had planned for you,
Miss Callanan, a ring so delicate
It would feel as thin as bridal lace.
Monsieur Billon and M. La Touche
Became, for you, rivals both
The way merchandise and love
Become rivals in a busy marriage.

M. Billon's delicate work I chose
As worthy of your gifted hand—
But today I searched high and low
From Drawbridge St to Bowling Green
For the ring that embodied how I feel.

My gift was lost in a gregarious moment—
Because I was drunk on wine from Pauillac
I cannot tell where the package fell.
Tomorrow I'll set the silversmith to work again,
A new ring to celebrate you; knowing full well
Nothing as delicate—by Billon or La Touche—
                    Can ever be assayed again.

He Turns to His Wife, 1797

You turn away from me in the fragrant heat
Of this Montenotte summer—
You are besieged with the bustle of parenthood,
More fatally besieged than I could ever be.

I watch the children cling to your waking hours,
Clinging as if their lives depended on you
For clean air, apples, for Olympian favours.
I am neither nurse or mother, but distant

With the precise tables of a marine clerk;
I am the scrivener, merely, of their triumphs—
Miss Callanan, I kiss the laurels on your shoulder
As you drowse beside me; you grown warm

With the radiant sandstone of August.
Your whippet lies lazy beside us, his black
Muzzle moist with dreams, your worn trug
Full of redcurrants overturned.

The heat of the city rises to our land
To sit upon your head like a crown.
Peace in our land, a peaceable Kingdom,
An English century seems peaceably to wind down

After the storms of regicide.
Ships out of France begin to trade once more,
The New World prospers.
A Murphy coaster skims the tide.

Ships like children attend to you,
Forever seeking you on the far shore—
Minerva in the summer's medallion,
Perfectly at ease after Mercury's wars.

He Feels Moisture Falling, August 1st, 1802

I think of my wife who attends to her sister,
Ill with the fever these seven weeks.
In the flat of the city every cess-pool is covered;
The poor are given fresh beddings of straw.
Now, the rain of St John's Day has dampened
Fires lit to ward off the feverish spores.
My own beloved, with the bravery of a sister,
Moves among the teeming crickets of the Marsh
While I have bedded in, a corncrake in the rain.

The summer corncrake that squeaks of loneliness
In these high fields of Joshua Beale
Has settled for life into a quiet backwater.
My wife says there is only one word for corncrake
And one word only that describes loneliness.
But it is August rain with its many words, sleet
And mist, hail and soft-fall, that has full dominion
Over the least of creatures, the unmusical corncrake.

He Spends Christmas at Clonakilty, 1809

Chilled to the bone at Ballinascarty, we took a glass of
    malt,
Headed westward then to my wife's dear town:
Snow as sharp as needles, an eastern wind,
Christmas in the promise of a blazing turf fire.

A doctor's child, my wife thinks of poor *spailpíns*
At this time of year, their unlit cabins at the roadside,
Hunger of the unwanted labourers we can see
From our quick-trotting four-and-sixpence day coach.

This Christmastide we have salted loins of beef,
Bacon and pullets, a roasted snipe,
And bread-stuffing bursting from the roasted goose;
Each garnish like a trace of small-pox on the skin.

He Buries His Father, 1809

The two old priests out of St Brendan's Parish,
One wearing his *bran-new* vestments,
The other a true friend of poor Henry Sheares,
Intone your name at the burial Mass:
You were the best father a merchant could have.

In all truth, it is as simple as that.
When I was a boy you established my right
To fish. You gave the Earl of Orrery hell.
You gave his friends, Deane and Bastable, hell.
A lover of life, you said a boy *must* catch salmon.

It was because of you I began to trade on water.
Our company's ships I see below Montenotte;
Their cargoes of iron rising from the polished decks
Remind me of the last salmon you gave my wife.
She cried when she saw your hands tremble

As your only son cries today. With trembling hand
You caught a fish, dear father. You stayed in my house
All evening, the three of us sharing the knowledge,
Like priests making the thurible charcoal blister
Or like blacksmiths upsetting iron at the anvil.

He Goes Through His Father's Belongings, 1809

Here are the seven letters from your wife when young.
She had just left the novitiate in France
Where she'd struggled to pray away her love for you.
Gentle, yet she was no respecter of language:
'Wasn't I the *amadán* not to see our *fíor-amour*?'
She needed to get home before words came apart:
The worst part of exile was the broken tongue

Though French life was deep in her Callanan heart.
Her own father was with Chevalier Dillon at Fontenoy,
Avenging his death at the Siege of Maastricht.
What is heroic about France gets lost in translation,
Except for this, her love-bond with the Dillon Brigade,
That, and the nervous memory of my father
When he waved goodbye on the road to Cove.

Her writing, now, is heavy and possessive,
Generous with all the ink of an exiled Sisterhood.
Lucky you, father: God couldn't hold her back.
Now the both of you are in the realm of archives
Where you can make peace with Kings and Prelates.

Her crisp stationery is frail in my hands, the edges
Roughly guillotined, the ink still Ursuline blue.

He Writes to His Estranged Sister, 1803

Beloved Letitia in Boston, forgive this trespass.
I met your own Pol's brother at the Mallow Spa.
He says you paint the birds of the New World

And that a son is born to you named Nathaniel Pat.
Though he be not the first Corkman born in exile,
I celebrate his birth. This September day

I have made cash deposits in his name—
Your Nathaniel Shea is now a capital Boy.
Though his fair mother gave her heart to birds,

Her New England son is now well-banked
In his ancestral harbour. May he come back,
With you, into his plumaged kingdom!

As for us, we prosper like pigs
In our city of silver-smiths and bacon.
European tyranny has been defeated for ever:

Unhappy politics is a scandal that's settled.
Now our lives are lifted by the prosperous din
Of priests at work, legal prayer, church repair.

He Walks with His Son, 1799

I walk with my boy in the flat of the city.
With his boots he kicks the salt of the ocean.
This is the way a child handles the flood,
Kicking it for the good humour, the laughter
Of flood water against King George's statue.

Sometimes I offer him my arm for comfort,
But he is too vain. He is a Catholic Hussar
On a five guinea horse. He is an Austrian.

'*Father*', he says. 'Father, frightened Pater,
I can see the line between the Mall and the flood.'

Floods. The sodden tea-chests worry me,
And fabrics out of Greenwich stained by salt.

Goods disembarked too soon are made vulnerable
While my son, unburdened, can tease the water-line.

He Mourns for His Nephew, Lt. Alan Mundy, 1814

The last time you went down the Jacob's Ladder
To make haste to the green and bitter sea
You eyed in disapproval the Admiralty's
Crofton Croker. We heard your secret laughter

Above the sound of waves. I see you ankle-deep
In Irish things, woollens, linens, music.
My Bristol nephew, you would dismiss or pick
Friends carefully, rejecting anyone cheap.

Brave nephew Alan, too young to die at sea,
Yet you sailed to the edge of our Empire.
It was you my good sister loved to inspire
With ballads from an Irish home in Nailsea.

When you were lost, in your twenty-eight-gun frigate,
You left us all, mere spars and cordage, barely afloat.

At the Annual Grand Masquerade, 1826

My youngest brother, who bought our domos
And tickets too, flirts with Mrs Jesse Whalen,
Sixty-two this week and beautiful
As the first day she sang at George's Street

Theatre Royal. Nothing is a killer of time
As love is. Mrs Whalen at nineteen years
Fell headlong for a Huguenot silversmith
And left my brother with such merchandise

As turns adulthood into a tragic art.
Sails badly torn, he continued to trade
Even in the sandbars and eddies of love.
Four sons now, two practising Law,

He cuts a dashing figure beneath the garlands.
Empowered by the Venetian mask of ownership,
He pretends no judgement is now being weighed
By this lovely assayer of the perfectly made.

He Meets His Future Sister-in-Law,
Miss Teresette O'Neill, 1811

My sister-in-law, late of Napoleonic Provence,
Carries six packets from her father's Italian days.
My brother is ill with joy. His bride so young,
His ageing fingers can hardly un-parcel gifts
Carried so deftly from the depths of France.
She is beautiful as the miniatures her father sent

And answers all the prayers a merchant ever sent
Heavenward. All the lavender of Provence
In her deep blue eyes, she is like France
After Revolution; bringing the red excitement of days
Into our grey offices. No merchant-ship ever held gifts
As beautiful. I barely remember love as young

As Miss O'Neill. Once, when I was under oath, young
And vulnerable in the church at Rome, misfortune sent
Me a passionate Trastevere girl. Her native gifts,
Her wifely love, drenched me like perfumes of Provence.
Seeing Teresette, so young, reminds me of those days,
As far away now as deep, blockaded France.

How fortunate of my brother, our agent long in France,
Certifier of old claret casks, to have found so young
A treasure. What spectacular luck in his tedious day
Of bargaining on the Bordeaux *quai*. Heaven-sent
Is Miss O'Neill; an unexpected treasure of Provence
Disembarking now at Passage with her parcelled gifts.

It is youth like hers, distilled in Europe, that has the gifts
Our troubled country needs. Wandering through France
One sees the uprooted and well-loved. Even in Provence
An exquisite Miss O'Neill, so vital and young,
Can hardly find a merchant house to nest. War has sent
Her into my brother's arms; war has filled his days

With her fragrance now. His autumnal, merchant days
Will be filled by her. I don't envy him these gifts
Suddenly arrived from France. War has often sent
Unexpected treasures to the rocks of Roche's Point. What France
Has made of Teresette is a miracle. She is so young
That all the merchants of Castle Street dream of Provence.

Days of Napoleonic colour draw to a close in France,
Yet gifts forever grow there. A land still young
With Revolution sent her here, fragrant as lost Provence.

He Considers His Wife's Three Cats, 1793

A different nation lives within our walls, cats.
Sent from God in triplicate, easy as envoys
Of a great power, my wife's cats enjoy the sun
As it fills each evening the bristling *chaise longue*.

I eye them in their un-translated power and they,
In turn, suffer me, a provincial merchant.
One rises like a green ceramic vase become liquid,
One sneezes neatly as if all the spice of Zanzibar

Had fallen upon her russet cloak. The cinnamon
Of their being fills their mistress's room
While I, mere man, could never coax such affection,
Such ecstatic welcome, from a Callanan woman.

Only some un-Christian force, primeval nation,
Could feed upon the certainty of human loves.
Cats upon cushions; envoys whose only purpose is
To stretch, to yawn in sequence, to be luxurious.

He Recalls a Letter from Home, 1771

Now there's nowhere cool to hide,
This late August in Rome.
A letter that has come to me
By kindness of
A Protestant landlord—
Owner of a Kildare estate,
Purchaser of Chevalier Piranesi's
Latest folio of stones—

A letter that sets my heart on fire
Provokes me to seek the shade
Of a wayward bergamot:
My Austrian Catholic cousin, John,
Has bled the family books
To death. A useless card-skill
Learned in an Austrian regiment
Has lost us to a Mallow rake.

One thousand guineas lost
At the Mallow spa
Has ruined four uncles
And my father too. Twice
Four hundred firkins
Bound for the Carolinas,
All auctioned off to save face,
To keep me in this, my Roman furnace.

He Considers the Rev. Dill-Wallace, 1817

This day my mind is full of the unhappiness
Of others.
In the heavy rain of afternoon
I receive a messenger
From that small home near Trinity Church.

I worry about Doctor Dill-Wallace,
My devoted friend and companion;
Sweet itinerant father of the Home Mission,
Unhappy now, like one disannexed and disgraced.

Though of the Romish faith myself
And friend of the four Capuchins in the Marsh,
I admire the Doctor's Bible-work
In the barbarous regions beyond Cork.

His winters in Corkaguiny
Among the aboriginals of Dingle and Ventry
Have yielded nought in the sight of God:
Each new light that made appearance
Seemed not to lift his Munster Presbytery.

This rain-drenched Eastertide
His Dingle flock has stoned him;
Sending him into undignified flight
Like Mr Knox who got a call from Alt.

In his letter he says he hears them still,
Crying '*Deontas! Deontas!*'—
The name of a strange Gaelic God.
This word has drained my weak friend
Who has lost quarter guineas in hundreds.

Their *Deontas* God has a hunger without end.

At the Grave of Amadé Dill-Wallace, 1800

October sun attends at the gate of your graveyard
As if October were the first soul
To greet Odysseus.
The world has gone under since Amadé died;
Your sweet boy trampled in a riot
Over the Union of our Kingdoms.

For this our hearts wear a wicked burden—
The endless canvassing of monies
With foreign peers upon the invaded quays.
It was the godless talk of favours,
Peerage and pocket-boroughs,
That fell upon your youngest child.

I am chilled by the grieving mother:
Poor Amadé, who so longed to travel north.
My heart is broken that he never saw Belfast.
Over her grief we should pour libations of wine,
Oils and perfume, first fruit of the South;
Something pure out of the antiphonal singing.

To our unhappy land I dedicate
His lock of jet-black hair.
Your little son, Amadé. Called after Heaven
Where love is. He is gone
To the pastoral charge of our history;
Through him the new century reposes in earth,
Nurse and mother of all things.

Rev. Dill-Wallace, you have caught a chill.
History weighs upon you
With the grief of abandoned fathers:
Though in a boy it is hardly history,
More the clear and personal tone of music,
The sound of a mother crying; grief's persistent noise
Like the long *kommos*
At Agamemnon's tomb.

He Collects His Framed Etching
of Cardinal Consalvi, 1823

Our Cork silver gleams in the afternoon sun
Of Merchants' Quay as I hurry to show
My son the exquisite work of Kean Mahony,
Beaten silver to frame the great Cardinal,
Saviour of Ferrara and Ravenna, hero of Rome.

No friend of the legations of men, no hero
Of the charcoal-burners, no light of the Marsh,
Poet of the Motu Proprio of 1816,
You were heaven's charioteer, Consalvi,
Through Napoleon's enlightened years

While the personal and minor anguish
Of our native land may never have touched
Your holy hand. Our hatred that is so local,
As intimate as the buckle on Metternich's shoe
Or the scent of coffee-beans burning

Near the Quirinal, that could never provoke
An Austrian frigate or the Corps of Murat.
Instead, my Franciscan nephew who sent the gift
Recalls the taste of burned coffee
On his lips and the laughter of an Italian child
As Lord Bentinck and Consalvi pass by.

He Prays to the Memory
of Cardinal Ludovisi, 1769

One thousand crowns a year.
At Castel Gandolfo, vineyard of the Irish,
I pause awhile with young Luke Cleary
And pray, Christ's humble *villeggiatura*,
To the Cardinal's sacred memory.

For who would befriend the Irish, wandering
As homeless Jews, but a will-full Saint
Of noble birth, unafraid of any embarrassment
We carry from the estrangements of defeat?
Sorrow was our great patrimony

To the Church of Rome. That, and some
Brains as bright as Luke Wadding or Hugh
MacMahon of *Jus Primatiale Armacanum*.
We pray aloud for princely Ludovisi's loss,
Pray the Seminarium Episcoporum of Rome.

He Contemplates His Failure, Rome, 1772

Midnight bells, tones of a thousand priestly tongues,
Cemeteries of a thousand martyrs,
Smells and consolations of a prison yard:
Nothing can console me for my loss,
The letter of failure that I signed to my father—

Angelica's sister, the memory of you,
How you hung about the College after Mass,
Unchaperoned by marriage, a lover in heat
For her Irish student-priest. I cannot forgive us.
Dirt on the road to Lucca

Reminds me of the unfaithfulness of flesh.
O married woman! Grief that I cannot tell.
I too was married and broke my vows
Between your Trastevere thighs.
You were schooled in the moist and naked

Places, you could twist and turn in the way
Of a young seal in Dunmanus Bay
Or sway like the strange minstrels of Christmas
In their Apennine costume. Mrs Furnari,
Principessa of mature loneliness,

You slipped by the old *custode*
Of the Torrione dei Venti and came to me,
Spirit of Santa Cecilia in Trastevere:
Of you, I feel the moist tremble still,
My fingers upon the spent *Kyrie* bell.

He Serves Mass at Advent, Rome, 1771

Even the incense of Christmas couldn't drown
Her scent, the smell of her as she sang to us
(Mr Barry and I). Her young sister, Angelica,
Took Mr Barry's breath away, but I held

My breath beneath a cascade of cloth;
So full of scent, so reckless for a scholar.
A poor cleric, how could I be loved like this,
All mouth and thigh? Terrible disgrace.

I think of the ambitious piety of my father,
Endless Franciscan prayers, Holy Father's goodness,
The Mass Rocks of Donoughmore and Clogheen.
Her mouth. Kissing her, I was the betrayer.

The thurible swings across my face,
Yet nothing in Rome can give me peace.
I came to Zion shouting, shouting for joy—
But it was with my father's breath,

His Sharon, his Glory of Lebanon.
Now, ambitious flesh has undone me.
Through the smoke of incense I see her thighs,
Angelica's sister kissing me, me inside,

And beyond the room where Mr Barry brought me,
The sound of laughter, Mr Barry's English friends.
Would that I be thrown from the Tarpeian Rock
For keeping company with their audacious art.

Memory

I

IT IS POETRY that constitutes our deepest memoir; and my sojourn at Rome—kept by me when I was hardly formed as an Irishman—is best remembered as an act of translation. Although my memories are of a time that is nearly fifty years past, the nature of nations hardly changes at all. As we have learned from the story of the Americas and the reshaping of Continental Empires, the structure of governments and kingdoms may change, but the people, even small nations, retain a continuity of character that seems immortal. Doges and Dukedoms may suffer historic humiliations, but Italy like Ireland never gives up the breath of its character. Italians are undoubtedly of a poetic and passionate temperament, with a limitless resource of music and an individualistic regional folklore. The popular poems and songs of the lower orders are numerous, and in general terms possessed of exceptional beauty. But the poems of the Italian nobility are a higher matter entirely. Here, the legacy of Tasso and Petrarch endures. High-born Italians, the nephews and nieces of Cardinals and children of Nobles and Ministers, are ablaze with the traditions of the soul. They are proud of emotion, and wear human feelings boldly like sashes of pure silk.

It was dear Mr James Barry, artist of immortal fame now cruelly expelled from the Royal Academy and Corkman in exile, who first introduced me to the poems of Count Luigi da Pora. 'What do you think of this mighty poem, Reverend Murphy?' Mr Barry shouted at me one day nearly fifty years ago in Rome, in the spring of 1769. With my clerical companion from Co. Tipperary, Luke Cleary, I had halted at the tables of the Osteria della Sybilla upon seeing Barry enthroned on a high chair of blue wrought-iron. At the time I was studying for the priesthood at our wonderful Irish College. I was not then equipped to withstand the company of fellow Corkmen, nor was I old enough to recognize artists and other occasions of sin.

With Luke Cleary tugging at my sleeve, I engaged in a long conversation with Mr Barry about the merits, indeed the grandeur and depth, of Count da Pora's work. A young nobleman born in Ancona whose father was originally from the city of Lucca, da Pora had spent a great deal of his youth in political agitation of one kind or another. On the very day that Mr Barry introduced me to his work the Count was travelling to Bologna in the company of an English noble-man to seek the release of his cousin who had been jailed for disturbing public order during the wedding of a Principessa of the district. In later years this same cousin would die in a political pistol fight at the foot of the Egyptian obelisk erected by Pius VI, the cultured Giovanni Angelo Braschi, opposite the Santa Trinita dei Monti. The perfection of poetry only serves to mask the reality of a country whose politics lies in ruins. Of the four poets of Italy transported by me into the cold journals of our Irish Kingdom, Count Luigi da Pora is truly glorious:

> The confessional prattle of wind
> Is sweetest gossip
> To the despised ranks.
> Sleet of sticks and stones

Whips the bare back-side of the garden,
As naked now as my poor knee,
In a torn Austrian collaborator's pants,
The bare weapon of a stone up my sleeve.

For all his political rages, and his Jacobin indignation at the injustices of the world, Count Luigi da Pora is essentially a poet of the heart. Sometimes his heart is that of a man darkened with rage, but even then his rage is never cold in the manner of a North European. His hatreds have the redemptive ease of pressed olives. I remember well our immortal Barry's enthusiasm for the Count's poetry, and his haranguing me for lacking in enthusiasm. 'Murphy, you Cork fool!' he shouted. 'You fool of a deacon! Can you not hear a masterpiece? These are among the greatest poems of the Italian language, a language in chains from the treacherous Bourbons who have suffocated Italy! Listen, Murphy!' And he recited the poetry in the raucous Italian of Roman streets, not the Italian of a nobleman or a priest. 'Is your family not connected with the printer Harris of Castle Street?' asked Mr Barry with all the emphasis and menace of a Blackpool tavern-keeper's son. Even then I was clever enough not to promise outright to have these poems printed in translation at my cousin's press in Cork, but I knew from Barry's murderous expression that he would hold me under an obligation to translate and publish these poets of Italy in the unfortunate kingdom of Ireland. It is a joy to me now, but also an unburdening of a promise to a fellow Corkman, that I have arranged for the printing of these translations of the poets of Italy at dear Mr Harris's shop in Castle Street.

Count da Pora's love of nature was a constant source of spiritual strength in a soul otherwise troubled with political conflict. It was for his troubles that Mr Barry loved him, I think, but the more astute literary printers of Ancona and

Naples defied Government orders and printed broad-sheets of his best nature poetry. Once I found Mr Barry weeping over a set of broad-sheets that had been recovered from the abandoned satchel of a print-maker's apprentice of Ancona. This poor apprentice of Le Marche had been bundled over a quay wall by a number of wild *ragazzi* of Rome. His satchel was purchased from the street urchins by the Dublin sculptor, Mr John Crawley, who subsequently gave the literary contents to Mr Barry and his English companions.

Ownership of these da Pora pages was like a sacred career, a holy office, to the impressionable, passionate and profoundly sentimental Mr Barry. The noble poet's peripatetic life, a wandering minstrel of revolution and fierce ideas, captured all of our dear Cork painter's heart and soul. An advocate and unappointed defender of every friend, Mr Barry would defend the reputation and literary brilliance of his Count to the very end. The printed pages that Mr Barry read from were covered with rough English translations and little cartoons of violent street incidents. The pages seemed an apt image of Mr Barry's world: a world of political poetry and symbolic death. I don't wonder now at the attraction of da Pora's work in the mind of our great Cork painter. The ever-presence of death, of personal destruction and political treachery, all transposed through the lyricism of Le Marche of Italy, struck a deep chord in the heart of our troubled Barry.

Count da Pora's poetry restores us to the physical reality of human flesh and human endeavours. He writes with the certainty that the poet's function is to be the nurse as well as the goldsmith of human life. There is a military physicality, a lack of decorous sentiment, in his expressions of love and general human intercourse. There is a seeming harshness in the vocabulary of da Pora, but it is a literary hardness that draws iron into the soul of the Italian language:

When I scooped
The fragments
Of our brittle love
From the floor
I couldn't—believe
Me—hurt a fly.

I felt as cleansed, then,
As a bloated monk
After an excellent
Session at stool—
As satisfied,
As angelic.

According to a note published in a Venetian literary journal, there is a little known detail of Church history associated with this particular poem. It is written that the irritable Neapolitan, Cardinal Sersale, might have beaten the simple Franciscan, Ganganelli, to the Throne of Peter were it not for the above poem of Count da Pora. An officer of the excommunicated Duke of Parma's household was heard reading this poem of da Pora's near where the fatal Conclave was meeting. Sersale, in a rage of Church orthodoxy, had the officer detained and questioned at length.

But it was history, and poetry—the true secret agent of History—that had detained Cardinal Sersale irrevocably. Thus detained, the Cardinal missed a crucial meeting with the Spanish Marchese Grimaldi and the support of the Bourbons fell to the future, ill-starred Clement XIV. Count da Pora's poem lost the Church not only a Neapolitan Pope, but, possibly, the Papal enclaves of Avignon, as well as Benevento in the Kingdom of Naples. It also lost the Church the immense salvation of Jesuit thought: in slandering the devout and blameless Cardinal Ricci and in proscribing the Society of Jesus, the Church amputated its own brain. Perhaps these things are God's Will, His test of our canonical intelligence.

Both Mr Barry and I were in Rome at that moment of spiritual darkness in the Church, when the Christ of the Franciscans, of beasts and birds, fell with a vengeance upon the Christ of manuscripts and grammar. I think the darkness of that intrigue never left the mind of Mr Barry. That incident rubbed a bitter vinegar into the canvas of his History painting. The doings of the Church had no influence upon da Pora, for he was a poet before his time, a kind of tyro-Jacobin. In his mind the doings of the Church were but part of the doings of mankind: he saw the Church as an agent of Kings and Imperial nations, a mere tool like a fast frigate or an instrument of war. In this I differ from him greatly: in truth, I had the greater advantage, having spent over two years in Franciscan contemplation while he fought and agitated for the freedom of his country and the restoration of his patrimony.

II

Even the elbows of bare trees creak
When the servants open the outer doors,
And sunlight in its little pantaloons
Runs barefoot, wanton, in the garden—

A FEMALE FRIEND of our great artist, Mr Barry, delivered the text of this poem to me at the Irish College. The woman's name was Angelica Centurioni and she appeared at the door of the seminary in the company of her married sister whose name was, I later learned with regret, Camilla Furnari. The Rector of the College called me to his room and I, a nineteen-year-old seminarian, was hugely embarrassed by the unsolicited attention of these attractive women. Despite my Cork innocence, I knew from previous encounters with Mr Barry that Angelica was his model and his mistress. But the presence of her sister, a married woman whose husband was a designer and maker of Church silverware, served to reassure the Rector who allowed me to take possession of the Barry letter and the manuscript of Count Luigi da Pora. The fine paper of the manuscript was embossed with the family crest of the da Poras. No doubt this also impressed my superiors. So much so, that in the presence of the women the Rector gave me permission to meet with Mr Barry at his studio to discuss the poem. By that time I was beginning to be treated exceptionally, an unhealthy arrangement in my spiritual formation; and one that would subsequently jeopardize my immortal soul and endanger my life.

But I remember well that day, in July, 1769, when my companion, Luke Cleary, and I walked with Mr Barry as far as the Vicolo delle Orsoline. We were all exhausted from the heat of Rome, but Mr Barry seemed particularly agitated. He claimed that his English colleagues were misrepresenting him in letters and verbal reports to his old patron, Edmund Burke. He said it was difficult for him, a red-blooded Corkman, to hold his tongue and maintain his composure. There was something deeply unworldly about Mr Barry's soul. Thought is the penance we do in this life, and his thoughts were full of the agitations and jealousies of artists and virtuosi in the *ghetto degli Inglesi*. He endured the competition, envy and the opportunist strikes of second-rate companions who had frustrated the sale of his work. At the time he was forming himself to be a great History painter in the manner of Michael Angelo or Raffael—the first such great painter of the British world. His being an Irishman only added spice to his brushes and made it likely that he would produce something more unconventional and sensational for the benefit of British life.

He was well aware of his origins in a merchant city of a small nation far away, a nation as vulnerable to the whims of great Empires as the enslaved citizens of Athens or the Papal enclave of Avignon. He had already copied three Titians and had, through such work, learned everything an Irish artist could learn about colouring. He defended yet again (as if he needed to solicit my nineteen-year-old good opinion) the potential grandeur of the artistic imagination in the Kingdoms of Britain and Ireland. Suddenly, he asked, 'What do you think of Count da Pora now? Is he not a genius? Have you studied the poem I sent to you by Angelica's hand?' I shook my head, for I had been rambling the streets of Rome since I took possession of the manuscript. 'Of course, you haven't,' he said. 'I must be mad. You've been walking these sun-baked streets with me. Come inside!' He gestured to the passageway that led into a darkened courtyard. Off this courtyard, up two flights of sandstone steps, was his great cave of Polyphemus, his chaotic studio that smelled of candle-wax and boiled mutton. He cooked while he worked, and this enraged his Italian neighbours who cannot abide capricious indoor cooks. Our Rector had once been called to the apartment of a man who had been stabbed to death for boiling cabbage indoors. Mr Barry at least had had the good sense to keep everything green out of his black pot, a pot that looked like the iron griddle of a Passage West fisherman's wife.

'It is da Pora's finest poem. He is the Rembrandt of Italian poetry, but he has done more for his nation than any artist I know,' said Mr Barry as I settled upon a seat made by stacking wooden frames and throwing what looked like a female garment over the construction. The apparatus creaked uneasily as I listened. I was alone, or, rather, I was the lone seminarian in this unconventional place because Luke Cleary had refused to come upstairs, but awaited me in the dark passage-way where street urchins ran and played. I watched Mr Barry intently as he spoke. He was not an elegant person, but a certain refinement crept into his manner as he spoke about the noble poet of action he admired. On an easel to his left was a luminous double portrait of a naked couple. The youthful locks of the pensive male were unmade and sat like a helmet upon the troubled youth's face. He held an apple in his hand, and another apple that seemed to have been incongruously cut in half by a knife lay at his feet. His companion, whose hair and toes and fingers were yet incomplete, looked at her would-be lover imploringly. One could see that a browned apple-leaf hid the masculine evidence of his excitement. This was Barry's *Adam and Eve*, a most sublime and compassionate work that was destined to find a permanent home at the Royal Society in London, a household companion to his immortal work *The Progress of Human Knowledge* in the Society's Great Room.

'Angelica, will you stand in,' Mr Barry suddenly addressed a shadowy figure in the darkness. From the shadows, behind my left shoulder, came a woman covered in a gold and black silk gown. I was astonished by the wealth of the cloak. To my untrained eyes it looked like a garment of fabulous value, something that might have been brought back by a trader of the Venetian fleet. Angelica, her hair undone and looking remarkably like the hair of the female in the double portrait, handed what looked like a bucket of ointments to the Cork *maestro*. 'A good mix,' he muttered upon looking at the concoction. 'Your hand. Your fingers, look at Reverend Murphy!' he instructed her. She looked at me. As she did so she dropped her cloak, revealing her completely naked person. At that instant I was too terrified to look away, for she had trapped me in her gaze as she was instructed. It was my first glimpse of complete female nakedness, a vision that I could never have imagined, although like any youth of nineteen I had had to banish many unformed and indistinct imaginary visitations of voluptuous ghosts. I gazed at her, not daring to move below her breasts, for she watched me watching her. But her bare neck and breasts were feast enough for a starved clerical student. I thought I would faint, with the heat, with the excess of her physical presence.

'I'm even more beautiful,' said a voice. It was Camilla, her married sister, now standing beside me, taller in her shoes. 'Mr Barry tried both of us, but Angelica has the rougher body, the more robust form—as the form of Eve must have been in those primitive, Arcadian days.'

'Though your body is more used, dear sister, having been spent in the service of marriage.'

'Hardly spent enough,' answered Camilla. 'My husband is a lover of silver, not flesh.'

'Here is a youth for you then, untried and *bran-new* like the Lord Mayors of Cork,' laughed Mr Barry. 'What do you think, Nathaniel?'

'Don't embarrass the boy, the sweet, sweet virgin,' Angelica complained. I could hear the annoyance in her voice, and I could see the sharpness of disapproval in her eyes. After all, she was his model. She, not her more elegant sister, was being offered up to the purposes of Art.

'That poem of Count da Pora's, speak it for the Reverend Murphy,' said the *maestro*. Camilla leaned across towards me and took the manuscript from my hands without asking. In prising them from my hands I felt that she had unbuttoned my tunic. I could smell her body odour, sweetened with a scent that must have been drizzled onto her bold bust. 'Yes, I'll read.' She drew herself up to her full height, a gesture that accentuated her bust: a most unusual preparation for the reading of a poem. And she read the words of Count da Pora beautifully: 'A parrot in a bishop's garb / Was preaching to a flock of birds . . .'

When she finished she gave a gentle bow, a gesture that once again exposed her perfect breasts. I turned away and looked at her naked sister, who was expecting my gaze. She met my eyes fully as if to say 'I know what you've seen. You want the touch of her flesh.' I tried to think of home, of the house of the Augustinians in Cork, of my mother who sent me abroad,—to the holiest place on earth, with the fervent hope of all her prayers that I become a pure agent of our despised Church in our troubled homeland. I withdrew my attention from these two temptations and recovered the authority of my vocation. Angelica was perceptive enough to notice the change that had come over me. Lovers of the mere flesh always deny the power of holiness, but constant prayer does bestow unimaginable powers upon the faithful. In a moment of prayer I was restored to the Church. Angelica, more humane and idealistic, broke away from the hegemony of her nakedness. She restored herself to her gown amid loud protests from Mr Barry, who complained that she was wasting his oils. She protested that her shoulders were aching. She needed a drink.

At this, this citadel of battle: I became aware quite suddenly of life as a struggle, a battle for integrity. The character of gallantry is never far from the heart of Count da Pora's work. There are many battles in his poems, or places of battle and places of sudden flight. He is designedly erring in his geography, juxtaposing images of the cold Lombard plains with the sun-dried terraces of Apulia and Sicily. There is within his work an abiding hero, a narrator at once liverish and loving, who confides in no one but the printed page. His narratives embody the night-flights of a later era, the coach-and-four escaping with the aristocratic patriot or the faithful husband. I tried to say these things to the company in Mr Barry's studio, but I felt that the beautiful sisters were no longer interested in me. I glanced at Angelica while speaking, but she would not meet my gaze. Her married sister had turned her back to me and was working at something between Mr Barry and the darkness. In turning away she had dropped the manuscripts of da Pora to the ground. A gesture of complete contempt: whether for me, for her sister, for Barry, I couldn't tell. Her gesture spoke of the darkness of her spirit. I longed to place my hand upon her shoulder, to tell her that it was not too late in our mortal lives to serve goodness, to beautify and adorn virtue. But I heard my mother's voice in my mind, yet again, and chose the quick discretion of flight.

'We shall see thee again, Nathaniel!' Mr Barry shouted as I turned and negotiated the darkened stairwell. As I descended I very nearly trod upon my cassock. I was relieved to see the happy face of Luke Cleary who had engaged a group of children in conversation. The children were laughing at something Luke had said and the sound of their laughter filled the courtyard with a thrill of innocence. I was grateful to God. Even now I find it difficult to call to memory the sensations of enchantment that the familiarity and warmth of these sisters had bestowed upon me. Nothing but fear had allowed me to thwart the inclinations of my body.

'What has happened?' Luke asked with alarm in his voice. 'Nathaniel, you look like a man who has seen a ghost.' I shook my head because at that moment I was incapable of speech. The manuscripts of Count da Pora's poems grew heavy in my arms, but I clung to them as if they were letters from home. The circumstances under which I came into possession of many of these singular Italian poems seem bizarre, now, from the perspective of this Safe Harbour on the cold Atlantic. But I have been provident with the stories of these poems. The story of how the poems travelled across a Continent ruined by war, the smells and texture of the foreign hands that handed them to me, have become part of the fabric of my possession of them. Their possession has been an inspiration to my own private poetry. Some of the detail within the texts, and, futhermore, some of the detail in my notes, may excite the unwelcome curiosity of minds that are provincial and prurient. As colleagues of mine will testify, I have been ferociously honest in my merchant life so that it will not surprise my friends to find here and there a blunt line or sarcastic comment.

The fact that I might have been a chronicler of that afternoon in July of 1769 was far from my mind as I walked the hot pavement back to the sanctuary of the Irish College. I could see that Luke Cleary was worried about me; as companions in the priesthood are always worried about some fearful and violent change. Camilla's words—not her sister's nakedness—haunted me.

> *Sunlight gushes forth from a cask*
> *That gleaned the heat from our hills*
> *Speckled with an abundance of vine.*

In truth, what can one say about such sublime poetry? The prevailing anxiety of Count da Pora's political activity was never allowed to circumvent the deep spirituality of his nature poems. Even the sunken dungeons of a Venetian prison, beyond the Bridge of Sighs where prisoners were brought to be strangled to death, could not weaken the resolve of our noble poet to praise the advent of spring in his native Le Marche valleys. It is part of the grandeur of his blood that his spirit thrived undiminished even when he was detained and threatened with a slow death by agents of the merciless Doge. The poet surprises us with the coming of spring, the strengthening sun that warms us is like an effervescent son of the family running through the garden. The Mediterranean February solicits our good humour and reminds us of the harvest of the grapes before winter set in. Count da Pora uses verbs as no Italian has used them: a succession of verbs becomes a sustained metaphor.

It is sunlight, February sunlight, that is the athletic infant of spring: sunlight is a wanton creature that captivates our awakened senses. Trapped between the Adriatic and the vast tracts of the Abruzzi, Count da Pora's childhood was a time of intense, familial contentment. Now, the pursuit of justice for his realm, the restoration of his patrimony, has become a cause of great bitterness of heart. Quite suddenly, adult life, for Count da Pora, has been filled with the pervasive sadness of politics. To understand this one has only to look upon the dispossessions and estrangements of our own native land to see what a fretful destiny is contained within public life. Such thoughts came to me as I thought of da Pora's exemplary bravery and sense of duty. He had endured torture in the sinking marsh district of Venice and he had longed so deeply for the places of his infancy while detained by agents of the Spanish occupation in Apulia. Yet he soldiered on, sending the brief lyrics of his indomitable spirit by couriers and common soldiers to the printing presses of Ancona or to the furtive political thinkers of Rome who sat in a permanent seminar of Orvieto and other cheap wines.

I thought, too, of the fractious exile of Mr Barry: how he had become a recipient of revolutionary favours. And of the women who surrounded Mr Barry, as all men who are agitated or touched by grief seem to attract the ministrations of the fairer sex. Thinking of those women, of Angelica and Camilla, brought further agitation to my disturbed and immature soul. A great sadness came upon me when I thought how foolish I had been to divide myself from the company of Luke Cleary, my dear and faithful companion. Images of nakedness oppressed my mind. I felt a primitive and melancholy need as if I belonged to the beasts of Mr Barry's genius. How could I have left myself open to such unorthodox encounters; although a great lover of poetry from early childhood, I am not a poet. Even now, after the settled intelligence of life has fallen upon me, I can see that I would have found great comfort and meaning in a life of priesthood rather than a life of poetry. In 1769 youthful desires rushed through my veins.

Melancholy seized my heart when I thought of the encounter at Mr Barry's studio. I was tormented by the threatening spectre of my own failure as a promising son of the Church. A stress had been placed upon my vocation, unfairly and with a certain orchestrated menace. In the days that followed I despised the company of artists and poets. I said many rosaries and offered up the most sophisticated *novena* of prayerful deeds to wash away the image of Angelica Centurioni's nakedness and the boldness of her married sister's words.

I despised the misery of Art. I contrasted the miserable dullness of the day-to-day life of an artist, the drudgery and anxiety of Mr Barry, with the sweetness and Christian kindness of the princely Cardinal Ludovisi, the Cardinal Protector of Ireland, who had donated his own money to the foundation of our College. I thought of the lasting memorial of this protectorate, the vineyard left to the faithful Irish at Castel Gandolfo and his one thousand crowns a year. Such bounty, such Roman generosity, and such a challenge to the weakness of our personal faith. Our little College had become the cradle of Bishops and Martyrs, a veritable Seminarium Episcoporum. The unworthiness of my feelings disgusted me. As the days passed it became very satisfying to forget everything of the world outside and concentrate on the task for which I had sought exile, the formation of my mind for the priesthood.

III

WEEKS WENT BY and I might have forgotten the world of Art in the embrace of the Church had the Rector not called me one Saturday morning. He wanted to show me something that had been delivered to the seminary. 'You see what acquaintances of yours have given to the College Library,' the Rector said excitedly. He pointed to a huge and luxuriously finished book of Roman prints that lay upon the table. It was the latest production of the Cavalier Piranesi: magnificent views of Rome, detailed and suffocating masses of rock, great columns of antique stone that served to humiliate and dominate the mere human spirit. 'The latest Piranesi,' he said, 'a gift to us from the Furnaris, the silver merchants. You have met Mrs Furnari in the company of that Cork rascal, Mr Barry.' He looked at me, expecting a reaction. 'You have met her, yes?'

'Yes. Luke Cleary and I met her in Mr Barry's company.'

'Wonderfully kind. Mrs Furnari was most impressed by her meeting with you.'

'It was brief. Mr Barry was working when I met him.'

'However brief, she was most impressed by you, Nathaniel.' I looked at the prints, heavy and dark. A Rome of menace, and a perfect metaphor for the menage that surrounded Mr Barry. I was silent and furious. The Rector interpreted my silence and my averted eyes as evidence of my interest in the Piranesi edition. 'Stay awhile,' the Rector said. 'Enjoy the book.'

I remained at the table, wrapped in silence, seething in rage. Something of the vigour of Count da Pora's poems entered my soul. I was politically angry like da Pora, I was betrayed like him and I could sympathize with his flights and his sufferings. Mr Barry had often told me how Count da Pora's work was little understood and appreciated in his native Ancona. According to Mr Barry, the literary circles of Ancona are difficult and hostile, with much stray and contradictory influence coming from Austrian agitation and opinion. As with many a port city where the dominant opinions are always imported, da Pora's genius would never be fully accepted by his own people. That is the lot of even the nobly born who endure the vicissitudes of commerce in a provincial city.

'Sunlight gushes forth from a cask / That gleaned the heat from our hills.' I thought of that wonderful phrase of Count da Pora's. It is so suggestive of light and fruitfulness; and faithfulness too, the fidelity that the vine shows to the earth and how the vine attracts the deepest heat of the sun: how the vine stores the heat for our future pleasure in the form of wine. I thought of these things, and I thought of the lightness of the valley of the Lee in my native land. The sweetness of the river Lee came to mind, its verdant banks and green hills that have rarely trembled beneath the onward charge of squadrons. Contrast that airy and sunlit landscape, the veritable Arcadia of my Cork childhood, with the dark dungeons of Piranesi's ruins; the inhuman scale of his imagination, and Rome that has endured the slaughter of ages.

Mrs Furnari. Camilla. What an uncommon attempt she has made to connect with me again. Me, her innocent Irish virgin priest, who was so stunned by the openness of her sensuous words. Now she would cultivate the good opinion of the Rector, a man of infinite kindness and human warmth. But how foolish he was to trust the character of every person. How easily an act of generosity, a mere printed thing, could capture the affection of a well-composed soul. He has been conquered by her, he has been taken by her, as I was taken—by the sound of her voice, the exotic promise in her words while I looked upon the nakedness of her sister. I felt keenly the strain of keeping her at the edge of my mind, but in truth she had broken through and stormed the inner ramparts of my prayers and habits. It has occurred to me many times that Italian women, so quickly roused to passion and jealousy, must also have those other skills—patience and discretion—since they live out their lives among a veritable herd of virgins. How strange it must be to wander freely as a married woman, knowing everything of the flesh, its stress and pleasure, among cloisters that are beaten down by the footsteps of those who are dedicated to loneliness. What privileges being the wife of a distinguished silversmith must confer upon her. She glides through congregations, between choirs and incense, with the spectral ease of a chalice. In my disorientated innocence I thought of her as a chalice, her moist lip touched by innumerable lips.

I turned the pages of the Cavalier Piranesi's book and marvelled at the frenzy of his ruins. How appropriate they seemed, those prodigious blocks that lay strewn upon the horizon as if some giant of the Classical era had dropped them while fleeing. How like my own soul the broken ramparts were, how apt was the image they wished to communicate. I thought how Mr Barry hated Piranesi's avarice, yet regarded him as the greatest of engravers and likely to go down to posterity with a deserved reputation. As I turned the pages a small spill of paper, light and porous as a piece of white cotton, fell to the floor. I stooped to pick it up. It seemed to have something written upon it. I took a closer look. Indeed, there was something written upon the communion wafer of paper. It was my name, *Nathaniel*, written in neat copperplate. Although I could not be sure, it seemed like a perfectly balanced script written by a female hand. Surely it was the work of Mrs Furnari's hand. I could hear her pronouncing my name.

Thinking thus of Mrs Furnari's script, I was reminded of all that work of scholarship, that aristocracy of learning, in the Italian world. Great poets of Italy have come not only from the high-born, but from the aristocracy of grammar that has ever been the consolation of the Church. First among all the scholar-Professors of the Irish College was the philosopher-poet Monsignor Limnio di Murthillo. He was born at Ravenna, the son of a senior army officer. He had all the bearing of a youth brought up in a military atmosphere, upright, restless, with his gaze forever on the horizon. Even when speaking to one intimately he never met one's gaze, but looked over one's shoulder like a sentry or a Sergeant of the watch on a Fort Camden tower.

Although in his early fifties when I knew him, he still had the rich raven-black hair of his Venetian mother. With the gift of hindsight, one can now place the achievement of di Murthillo squarely between those two more famous Italians: the Milanese, Fr Giuseppe Parini, and a fellow-poet of Ravenna, the duplicitous and opportunist Vincenzo Monti. Indeed Monsignor di Murthillo knew the Monti family intimately and encouraged the young Vicenzo in his studies and his poetry. Monti repaid the Monsignor's kindness by becoming a republican when it seemed that the Republic and its avaricious citizens would take over the Roman states. Monti's ode 'Al signor di Montgolfier' is merely the retelling of an early unpublished work of Monsignor di Murthillo, a work that I heard the Monsignor recite in the library of the Irish College on one St Patrick's Eve celebration. I know the Monsignor idolized the sublime Parini. Parini's 'Il Giorno', with its masterly components, 'Il Mattino' and 'Mezzogiorno', had a profound effect on its readers: this satirical account of an elegant and infatuated, idle and attractive noble Milanese youth swept across the quiet libraries of Italy. Didactic and ironical, the great poetic work contains within it a new kind of thought—a sense of social justice and an attack on the attitudes of the Old Régime.

Although he was neither a republican or a Jansenist heretic of the Austrian kind, Monsignor di Murthillo's eyes and ears were open to the sufferings of the poor and the lower clergy. He had the courage of a Lord Edward FitzGerald or a Robert Emmett. He was quick to represent the interests of some unjustly punished priest or deacon to the higher echelons of Roman society (to which he had quick and easy access). In later years, mainly, it is said, to monitor and undo the damage done to truth by the upstart Vincenzo Monti, the Monsignor cultivated the friendship of Cardinals, patrons, the inebriated members of the Accademia dell'Arcadia as well as art-dealers and *ciceroni*. He knew the Prefetto della Antichità of the Vatican, the famous Johann Winckelmann, and it is said that they spent many hours together at the workshop of the sublime Bartolomeo Cavaceppi. He had had a serious quarrel with Cavaceppi after the death of Winckelmann, an estrangement that was never healed. He never forgave Cavaceppi for his encouraging Winckelmann to travel northwards after the Seven Years' War. It was on the homeward trek of that journey that the great scholar of Ancient Greece was murdered for the sake of a few medals presented by Empress Maria Theresa. Winckelmann was to art what our own Edmund Burke was to politics: he pursued the noble simplicity and quiet grandeur of entire civilizations and he knew that beauty was one of the greatest mysteries of nature. Like Monsignor di Murthillo, he understood that we were not savages because we could study Greek.

CASALBORSETTI

Afternoon at Casalborsetti,
I forget for a moment the cradle of home—
So many strangers at this seaside place,
Dressed to perfection against Adriatic rain:
They are disgorged from carriages,
The Visigoths and Arians, Barbarians
And the children of Honorus;
Odoacre and Theodoric:
The common hordes of Europe take root.
At Casalborsetti despair takes hold,
Like a mist creeping up the San Vitale pines.
This place is full of victories and retreats,
And I, an amnesiac priest of daily office,
Recall the day an idler wrote upon the quay
'Run to the sea if you have a palette of pigments':
An irony lost in a fisherman's dialect,
And obscure to all Regiments of the Austrian North.

I shake off the Casalborsetti mist of despair:
Back in Ravenna there is a bed for me, I know,
In that wilderness of walls, that beehive of mosaic—
If another Baroque apse were offered I would go.

Monsignor di Murthillo's work is distinguished by its local piety, its sense of the rightness and solemnity of local life. That view of life both familial and scholarly is a seeming contradiction in his work. But that is his true nature, his signature in the great world of Italian letters. In 'Casalborsetti', for example, he celebrates that elegant and bustling fishing village near Ravenna where he spent many childhood summers. Yet this poem is not merely a description of Le Marche pines and Adriatic rain: it is a catalogue of the nations and civilizations as they took root in that intimate childhood place. 'A Trastevere Flautist' is again more than that mere description of a Roman street musician. It is both a celebration of Rome and a description of the excited force of Roman music. Few Italian poets have di Murthillo's depth of soul. The philosophical depth of the Monsignor can be gauged today by perusing the pages of old Italian journals where di Murthillo published his thoughts in brief paragraphs, all under the working title *Living Questions*. His day-by-day journalism has been a healing force in Italian religious life. It has raised the level of discourse, and taught the truth of God's goodness to both Rome and the enemies of Rome. When he writes of 'music at the core' he means more than the temporal sounds of this life. He means the echoes of heaven.

Our own Mr Barry thought little of Monsignor di Murthillo. There was within Mr Barry a fierce capacity for intellectual jealousy or, at the very least, a tendency towards undeclared rivalry. 'Has your Monsignor created any more Bishops for martyrdom in Ireland,' Mr Barry teased me one day at his table in the Osteria della Sybilla. He liked to ignite my faith and to watch the full conflagration of an immature and youthful vocation. He knew that the Monsignor was a friend of Winckelmann, the philosophical enemy of British painting. He knew also that the Monsignor had worked tirelessly to direct the more intelligent Irish students toward the mission in Ireland rather than into the fold of the Jesuits. An innocent abroad, I always rose to Mr Barry's bait. But he admitted—as did Mrs Centurioni, who always had opinions on such matters—the genius of di Murthillo's poetry. The Monsignor was also an *improvisatore* of great renown. He could recite the lengthiest and most complex poem instantly on any given subject. Once, when challenged by an Austrian Cardinal, he recited three hundred well-turned verses on the subject of Veneto cheese. His mind was crammed with the resources for impromptu poetry, from the Latin and Greek texts of the Ancients to the verses of Ariosto, Tasso and Petrarch.

FATHER

Through my long priesthood I have seen you
Under the submissive harness of labour—
Your peasant jacket at the kitchen,
The thinnest slices of Parma ham.
Back in the days before the Regiment
You were a follower of the plough.
I recall the pride in my breast
When you showed me the red wax of nobility,
That call to arms as the Duke's officer;
And those veteran years, the grey acquiescence
After battle, the grey cloud of the unwanted,
Those dark squadrons of unnecessary men
Gathering at Ravenna, the graves
Of martyrs at your back, the camp followers
Who starved at the harbour front.

Although the friend of Cardinals and Dukes in later years, di Murthillo never forgot the humble origins of his strict and militaristic father among the woodcutters of the great pine forests north of Ravenna. He remained deeply loyal to his family, but particularly proud of the stoicism and simplicity of his father who had brought honour to the men of Ravenna in a succession of marshland battles. The elder di Murthillo retired with the rank of Colonel, but retained the modesty of a private soldier throughout retirement. It was this modesty of origins that Monsignor di Murthillo shared with Johann Winckelmann who was himself the son of a Prussian soldier. 'Of late I find patches in your shoe' is typical of that prayerful admiration that the Monsignor has shown towards the elders of his family. Wealthy from an unexpected trade in Venetian glass, the di Murthillo household maintained its social kindness and its demotic sense of the world. The family became an ornament to society in Ancona, yet never an ornament in that facile and falsely gilded sense; rather, ornaments as a source of light, for the family has produced a clutch of brilliant intellectual children, many of them widely published. 'Nothing is left uneaten': this surely is the telling line of a di Murthillo. In his work every hour of life is surveyed and every line that's written strikes home.

The warm architecture of family and ties of blood are dominant themes in the work of di Murthillo. The above poem has been published in two versions in Roman journals. I have compared the published versions of September, 1768 and April, 1771 for the purposes of my translations. It astonishes me that I first worked upon these translations over thirty years ago, yet I cannot fix upon a settled version of any work by di Murthillo. I can only bring news from the world where the poems fully reveal themselves. In this poem our Monsignor praises the ordinary people of Le Marche: country people with grace and style, and with that effervescence and innate mischief so commonplace in the Italian countryside:

Your husband, Tommaso, nudged my ribs
For every beauty making her promenade.

73

You were the suave authority of the palace—
Without license wandering the corridors,
Waking us children before dawn.
Once, we hunted truffles in the woods,
Baskets in hands, on your little mule.
I was embarrassed to walk beside you
When the animal struggled with its load.
Once we reached the epic funghi
After I was trapped in a lattice-work of vines—
That was in the estate of Amerigi nuns.
Children floated in the pool of the mendicants,
Their arms and legs a tangle of weak vines
Combed fine by the care of Ravenna nuns.
When touched by water they flashed like beavers,
Their lives being buoyed by the oils of care.
The lattice-work of vines fell from my eyes.
It is true I didn't care, in a curate-like way,
For your uncouth hair, your worn tunics.
But, Isabella di Murthillo, I know
You ignited this love of anointed things,
Greek statues of childhood; weeping stones that heal.

Translation is an imperfect art, and it should really only be used for the purposes of trade and diplomacy. Having lived in Italy for a number of impressionable years I can now say confidently that it is the *reader* and not the *text* that requires a full translation. To understand the work of Monsignor di Murthillo one would have to be a complete Italian—there are nuances and a thousand associations, both linguistic and political, which cannot be captured in the English tongue. Every translation is a fraudulent report upon an event that has happened elsewhere. Poems, especially, are anointed things. Poems contain spirits and chrisms visible only in that consecrated place of making. To disturb a poem into another tongue might seem a desecration of some kind, yet the effect of its holiness is something that *can* be transported to the port of another tongue.

'You ignited this love of anointed things.' The above work is one of my wife's favourite poems. A man cannot bestow higher praise upon a work of art. Indeed, this particular poem may have helped me to capture the love of my life, my beloved wife Louise. While negotiating a cargo of linen and butter for Lisbon with her father I happened to let fall these poetic papers of the Italian world, my scrambled work of translation, upon the floor of their Clonakilty counting-house. It was Louise Callanan, then but nineteen years old, who scrambled to the ground to retrieve them. She was fascinated by my Italian sheets and my scribbled English versions. After dinner at her father's house that evening, she extracted a full explanation from me. I was then thirty-seven years old and those memories of Italian life were already dimmed by the frantic exigencies of the Atlantic trade. At thirty-seven I was a hardened and efficient Cork merchant, having extracted my father and cousin from the Debtor's Court with the aid of seven Venetian diamonds. I had rebuilt the family business, and nothing hardens a man more.

When I departed from Clonakilty on the following afternoon Louise had reserved several pages of my work to herself, but also the more intimate facts of my own personal poetic efforts: facts that I had never shared with anyone to that day. Through the summer of 1787 Louise corresponded with me. I remain profoundly grateful to her liberal parents—persons of the utmost respectability among the professional classes of West Cork—who didn't intervene in our strange correspondence. By that time I had leased my own properties in Montenotte as well as the offices at Penrose Quay so that Miss Callanan began to visit me at home, accompanied always by her gracious mother. I associate all of Monsignor di Murthillo's poetry with the heightened blessings of those early days. Louise and I decided to marry almost upon our first meeting. I was keenly aware of her youth and my crusted maturity, and aware too of how a young woman who marries a man too far advanced from her in years is but storing for herself a companionless old age. But love lies a-waiting for all of us; of this I am certain. At nineteen years of age, Miss Louise Callanan walked into my settled and bleak life and assumed complete authority over everything in it. We were married within the Twelve Days of Christmas, on January 2nd, 1788, by an affable and obliging Canon Healy-Ford, a cousin of Louise's gracious mother, Kitty.

IV

As I compose these notes, now, on the day of our thirtieth anniversary, I give thanks to God, Our Father in Heaven, who held this treasure in trust for me. I recall the wretchedness I felt at the loss of my vocation after a disturbing carnal moment or two at Rome. But let no one misunderstand my notes: my own Louise of thirty years' companionship is the complete beloved of my heart and soul. (One needs to state these things plainly for in printing these words at Castle Street there is every certainty that they shall fall into the hands of Mr Atkinson's Boston readers who do not know me personally).

One can see that festive and crowded atmosphere of life in each one of di Murthillo's poems. The mischief of family, the loyalty of aunts and uncles, the faithfulness of fathers, all pour into that anointed space of his imagination:

> *A tobacco-pipe drooped from your lips*
> *As I trailed after you through the palace.*
> *I was the grand vizier of palace dust,*
> *Not always held in high esteem.*

Expressions like 'palace dust' and 'childless rooms' function as metaphors for worlds where the blood of family is absent.

Many Italian commentators, at least those who were still allowed to publish during the Napoleonic occupation, have interpreted the 'family' in di Murthillo as a metaphor for the scattered and threatened Church during the Empire. Accused of unpatriotic tendencies by the communes of Genova and Torino, the work of di Murthillo has been torn from journals and his collections removed from all civic libraries. But I see his work as something utterly beyond politics. The destinies of Government are beyond him as they lie beyond every effort of refined imagination. A poet can only embody politics, make metaphors of history and power in the manner of a canvas by Mr Barry. But words are a poor and easily penetrated substitute for the colours and sealants available to the great painters. Lacking a finished and protective varnish, a poem may be freely entered and misinterpreted by any member of the world's laity. Perhaps it takes an entire generation for the true finish of a poem to be formed. Politics has no such patience, and this philosophic difference has led to the flogging and death of many poets. Indeed, we have seen poets hanged in our own country.

It is a little known fact that di Murthillo was an intimate friend of the hapless Clement XIV. The Holy Father's reckless habit of dazzling prelates and ambassadors with a mirror as they walked in the gardens of the Quirinale can be directly attributed to Monsignor di Murthillo. The Monsignor had an especial relationship with mirrors, formed as a boy when a Venetian ship foundered on the mud flats near Casalborsetti. The ship, bound for the islands of Greece, had been carrying a cargo of mirrors from one of the great Murano manufactories. The entire cargo was spilled into the Adriatic before the eyes of young di Murthillo and his fellow villagers. In his memoir published by the Diocese of Ravenna, the Monsignor has described the 'sea of mirrors' that lay before him, the light dancing upon Adriatic waves, fish trapped and leaping from the brilliant surface of mirrors when waves receded, and the entire luminous shore that became unbearably crowded with reflected light. When di Murthillo first came to Rome he brought with him nearly half a coach-load of Venetian mirrors that had been finely re-crafted by his cousins in Ancona. One can still find di Murthillo mirrors in the best drawing-rooms of Rome and Lazio. Thus, one can understand why di Murthillo and the frightened Pontiff were to be found dazzling the Ambassadors of Europe from the safety of Clement's apartments. I have recently seen a Maynooth-published note of poor Pope Clement addressed to di Murthillo: 'Ah, Limnio, we have spent our best days in idle *speculum*.' Clement XIV's papacy was a brief one, and, indeed, a poor reflection upon the wisdom of the Church.

Di Murthillo's line reminds us of the Casalborsetti evenings of his childhood and the Ancona beauties who used the Adriatic light as that perfect frame for their attractive youthfulness. He contrasts youth with family, adventure with faithfulness, so that his best poems of memory have within them a human as well as a philosophic tension. His poem also contains a poignant tribute to the Sisters of Amerigi who took it upon themselves to rehabilitate and educate the homeless and handicapped children of Le Marche. 'After I was trapped in a lattice-work of vines' reminds us of that common sight of the Italian countryside, the swelling clusters and luxuriant tendrils of vines that spread wildly over a lattice-work of hedge-rows. In more sophisticated vineyards of Italy the vines are borne aloft by growths of Elm, Elder and Maple, thus freeing the ground itself for the double production of wheat and grass and vegetables. The sight of such enclosures as one passes through Italy in early summer leaves an impression of immense fertility and intense husbandry. At such times Italy takes on the atmosphere of a Garden of Eden, a land that has been formed by God Himself to teach us North Europeans what Heaven must await the saved and the faithful of the cold North. Having been born Italian, how idle it is to proclaim that Heaven does not exist. How difficult it must have been in the decades that followed the Pontificate of Clement XIV for those Patriots and Republicans of Italy who had to endure the support of those who proclaimed that God was dead. When Pache and Hebert and Chaumette declared before the Convention that the worship of Reason was to be substituted for the Love of God, the vines of Italy never ceased to produce their bounty. When Notre Dame was declared a Temple of Reason only an actress could be substituted for the Madonna. Even Robespierre himself became disgusted with the atheism of the Commune. It is wonderful to think that Monsignor di Murthillo and many poets of the spirit survived through the imprisonments of two Popes, Pius VI and Pius VII, as well as the seizure of the Papal States, the Concordat of Fontainebleau and its Annulment, and endured to witness the triumphant return of the Holy Father on May 24th, 1814. One of my treasured possessions is a letter written to me in triumph on that fateful day by Bishop Luke Cleary. Luke had just ordained twelve priests for the Mexican and American missions.

CAVACELLI'S GREEK DANCER

All we desire is to be with you, dancing,
High upon the pedestals of Rome.
We were numb as Prussians,
Mere simple Stendal cobblers,
In your marble presences—
So that our neo-Classical phrases,

Everything Winckelmann and clever,
Couldn't find purchase, couldn't succeed;
Couldn't succeed as the heart does
In your marble presences. Cavacelli,
Cavacelli makes the heart sing; a chorus
Of water ripples back to Greece
When your mind imitates everything Greek,
When you set the apprentice fingers
Working overtime, heart in hands. Our Roman
Minds are so full of love they become a book:
'Thoughts on the Imitation of Greek Works.'

In the above poem di Murthillo offers the most complete and
sublime praise of the work of Johann Winckelmann as well
as enfolding within the Classical philosophy of the Prussian
Keeper of Antiquities at the Vatican that moment of dance,
that poetic choreography of Roman life. All of the human
traffic of Rome is embodied in the marble presences of his
mutual friends, the philosopher and the sculptor. (Many visi-
tors to Rome remark that Cavacelli was a mere copyist, but
Winckelmann understood that to copy and reduce Classical
statuary is of itself an effort of scholarship and art.) In this
poem we are in the sublime territories so well documented
by Mr Burke and so effortlessly catalogued by Winckel-
mann. While Rome has had to endure the manifold vexa-
tions of tourism, it has only recently learned to interrogate
its own monumental face. By the middle of the last century
the traffic of strangers had been an immense intellectual
benefit to Rome. Fresh air of North European curiosity had
blown across the settled and sometimes putrid waters of the
Tiber. Until that influx of foreigners Romans had very little
interest in the genius and intellectual creativity of elsewhere.
Even in the field of literature, so mobile and readily commu-
nicated, the native Roman spirit was both repetitive and

decadent. Everybody wrote in Rome, from bakers to Cardinals, from grocers to Monsignors. There was an intense pseudo-Classicism, fake Pindars and Virgils, dreadful sonnets and tragedies. Venerable bodies were constituted with the most complex rules and hierarchies. Indeed, Monsignor di Murthillo spent a great many hours in courteous dishonesty with the more distinguished members of these literary sodalities. Their seniority ruled the roost, so that a poet of real merit and critical insight was undermined and silenced by the sheer bulk of their mediocrity. Even the Accademia degli Arcadi with its self-proclaimed mission of purifying Italian poetry was merely a puffed servant of orthodoxy. There was, also, a complete obsession with Rome itself, with birthright and citizenship and the primacy of the place's imaginative superiority to everywhere else in Italy. This led to a hopeless provincialism in literature; a determined lack of interest in the talents of others. It was impossible to sell the poetry of a poet who was not from Rome. There was no interest in Alfieri or Gozzi, and even the greatest Italian dramatist of the era, Goldoni, saw his productions fail at Rome. In this atmosphere, some banker or grocer was sure to remark that he could produce better plays himself if only he cared to apply his valuable time to the task. This is the sure sign of a provincial tyranny at work.

Our own di Murthillo navigated the ship of his prodigious talent through these unpromising waters. He knew the one great Roman-born author, Pietro Metastasio, who also glided like a veritable trapeze artist above the mediocrity of the streets. He avoided the conclaves, the hierarchies and the pompous titles so assiduously fought over by those who are second-rate. He avoided the pitfalls of those parodies of Platonic idealism and produced dramatic commentary that has the grandeur and force of Racine. Because of the traffic of personal poetries there was a great illusion of intense literature. Here, even a tolerable Greek scholar might be declared a genius and invited to all the important salons of the city. This atmosphere left many despondent, but not Winckelmann, nor di Murthillo, nor the industrious and inspired Cavacelli who worked honestly at his workshops and provided a meeting-place for all who were discerning and curious.

It should be noted that music was the exception to all that pervasive mediocrity. The Sistine Chapel and the Congregazione di Santa Cecilia controlled all the music, sacred and profane, that was heard at Rome. And it was music of the greatest melody and taste, played upon sublime instruments and amplified by the greatest choirs ever heard in Europe. I shall never forget the first time I heard Gregorio Allegri's wonderful *Miserere*; a performance made even more memorable when the guardians of the choir apprehended a musical father and son from the Austrian Court who were found copying the music as it was sung. I still have four sheets that fell from the younger thief's hands as he made the quick getaway of a common blackguard. It was with choral music that Rome achieved the incandescent likeness of Heaven and as a young priest in training I imagined the perfect harmony of choirs cresting above the vineyards and enclosures of Italy. It was with music, surely, that the Mater Ecclesia hastened forward to embrace those of personal faith. Even today, when I am detained at the Custom House or halted for a change of horses at Clonmel or Macroom, the sublime music of Rome washes over my spirit so that my illuminated heart becomes a willing refuge for all the dethroned monarchs of the last century. It is a politically untenable moment for a rebel Corkman, of course, and it soon passes.

V

I FIRST READ Monsignor di Murthillo's poems in an ecclesiastical journal published at Ravenna in the summer of 1770. It so happened that less than a fortnight before Luke Cleary and I were due to travel out of Rome for our annual *villeggiatura*, the College Rector sent both of us on an errand to collect a package at Cavacelli's workshop. In was a warm day in mid-summer, such an afternoon as one that would cause Romans to extend their sojourn indoors and keep the shutters unfolded against the heat. But Luke and I were glad of the chance to walk in the districts beyond the Irish College, to taste that rancid atmosphere of the world of the laity. Luke and I were in high spirits at that time for we had been exceptionally chosen to carry the *baldacchino* for part of the way when the Holy Father carried the Blessèd Sacrament at the Corpus Christi procession. We had acquitted ourselves very well, so that the Rector was proud of us, temporarily at least. The package at Cavacelli's was but a bundle of books and journals, including the journal that contained di Murthillo's verse. Luke and I perused the texts, of course: we never awaited the permission of the Director of Formation, but read everything and absorbed everything. This congenital lack of respect for authority, lack of fear in the face of established procedures and protocols, is particularly

Irish, I think, and comes from the bitter experiences of history. The status quo in our country has never been associated with our best and common interests, so that we apply a belligerent scepticism to all rules and regulations. Now that he is a Bishop, I am sure that Luke has a much higher view of authority and discipline, but in truth, in 1770 we were both equally barbaric and intractable. We stood outside Cavacelli's workshop, amid a crowd of distinguished and aristocratic-looking visitors, and took our ease in the sun with unlicensed texts from Ravenna.

At that moment we were hailed by a familiar voice: 'Father Murphy, you young scoundrel!'

It was Mr Barry, bearing down upon us in a flurry of capes and rags and rolled canvas. 'I have just been holding forth upon you and your cousin, the printer Harris. Have you written to him about the great poets of Italy? I have received more of Count da Pora's poetry. What have you got there, are those journals from Cork?' I told him the nature of the books in my possession, a piece of intelligence that was hardly his business. However, he was a great artist, and, more to the point, a fellow Corkman. I showed him these new poems by di Murthillo, in particular 'Cavacelli's Greek Dancer' that I thought of as sublime work. Mr Barry distributed his burdens between Luke and myself and took temporary possession of our package. He hummed and grumbled as he read the poetry. 'Bah, nothing like the Count da Pora. Where is the passion for life? Where is the struggle?'

'Show me your Count's poems, then,' I answered boldly. I would not be patronized, nor would I, even then, allow di Murthillo's work to be patronized.

'Let's walk together. I need to quench my thirst. My throat is still wounded. I have been afflicted by a series of terrible fevers. People are trying to poison me here, I can tell. The place is a nest of poisoners.'

We turned and walked briskly with him to the Osteria della Sybilla, his favourite haunt. Mrs Centurioni was at the table, having awaited his return. She rose to greet us, not in the least surprised at Mr Barry's companions. Mrs Centurioni looked beautiful that afternoon, lush black hair and that vibrant, demonstrative beauty of Roman women. Mr Barry had spent seven weeks copying another Titian. His fourth Titian, he said, as if the canvases of the great painter were but horses that he had ridden. He said that he was forming himself to be a great History painter, the greatest painter of History in England. 'In London I won't be jostled down by too much competition, Nathaniel, for the great genius of English painting is in portraiture, not History. Coming from Cork gives me an edge, boy, it gives me an added dimension as real and weighty as a great store of sulphurs and intaglios.' He explained to Luke and myself that our unhappy Irish history had left us with deep wounds in our character, wounds that made us seem historical in the manner of the French or Italians, even as we lived and breathed. He said that an Irishman's appetites would never be sated by mere portraiture or any form of domestic auto-biography. Mrs Centurioni stroked his face as he spoke and ostentatiously tried his brow for fever.

'I'm done with Rome,' Mr Barry said, startling even Luke who was not too agitated by these artistic things. 'As the prosecution of my plan to be the greatest History Painter of England depends largely upon the antique and nothing else on this earth, I mean to raise twelve guineas, thirty zequines, mind ye, by which I might have some of the greatest anti-quities moulded off and the casts sent to Cork or London. Dr Sleigh was to come here bearing gifts, but he has become a Doctor of Betrayal. Traitor to a fellow Corkman, I tell you, you poor Deacon of Superstitions.' He took a wild swig from the flask of Orvieto that had been placed on the table. 'My enemies have got to him. I'm sure of it. Since I came to this noble place I've been surrounded by enemies. They have tried to carry my name away from the affections of Mr Burke. They have succeeded in allowing me no profit from my art, not one zequine.' He lowered his head in a show of grief. Not a noble head, I thought at the time, not nobly born but churlish-looking, peasant-like. But his genius was noble. His mind was made beautiful by history, especially the history of Greek painters whose character he had re-imagined for himself (and for all who would listen) from the mere fragments of the Greek world that lie scattered like ghouls in the great caverns of Cavalier Piranesi's prints. In this moment of sadness Mrs Centurioni moved over to him and caressed his head like a mother, her raven hair falling over the distressed genius. He suddenly raised his face and took Mrs Centurioni roughly in his arms, kissing her hungrily. His hand was upon her breast. Both Luke and I were shocked by such licentious behaviour.

'We must go, Mr Barry,' I said, as gently as I could.

He laughed at me, pressing his hand more deliberately upon his lover's breast. 'Now, Reverend Murphy, put that in your next letter to Cork. Let them read of my scandalous life at Rome. Let them know that Blackpool has given birth to a genius!'

'We *should* go,' Luke said, tugging at my sleeve.

'Hold your station!' shouted Barry. 'You haven't seen my latest versions of Count da Pora. Sit awhile, Deacon Murphy, you will not lose your immortal soul by poetry alone!'

But we made to go, for we felt that the poor genius was unstable at that moment and might cause an incident that would excite the curiosity of the police. 'Luke has been translating the Principessa Nulana Nigonelli,' I say quite suddenly, just to distract the artist.

Luke looked at me in disbelief. Now I was a betrayer.

'"A fish leaps into a woman's bucket." I remember that line, immortal lines!' shouted Mr Barry. 'A slip of a girl who sailed away with a merchant of the East. What a destiny for a poet, what a destiny for a Princess! What can the line mean, what can it mean?' He plunged his hand between Mrs Centurioni's thighs in a gesture of wanton and scandalous vulgarity. Mrs Centurioni screamed, but with delight, for she turned and kissed the artist's mouth. We turned to leave, but Mr Barry shouted after us 'My brother is dead, dead in Cork, I tell you!'

'Which brother, dear Mr Barry?' I asked, for I knew the family. 'Do you not have three brothers?'

At this, Mr Barry began to weep. 'I don't know, dear Nathaniel. I don't know which brother. Dr Sleigh did not say which brother. Cruel Sleigh, cruel, cruel Sleigh. He has not lifted a finger to help me.' At this he began to weep once more. Mrs Centurioni was weeping and muttering words of consolation. They had both taken much to drink. It was understandable. What a dreadful, partial letter to receive from Ireland. Not knowing which brother, a man would be forced to grieve for all. 'Here, take these,' Mr Barry, through a mist of tears, looked at me. He handed me the sheets with new poems by da Pora. 'Take them. Send them back to me at this Osteria.' He dismissed me and Luke, and we turned to go.

'You should not have mentioned my translating,' Luke admonished me as we hurried back to the College.

But I was too upset for poor Mr Barry to be upset for Luke. I did think of the beautiful, finely etched poetry of the Principessa. I thought of the two or three poems that Luke had recited in the Rector's library, translating by sight, committing nothing to paper.

With di Murthillo in the Ravenna journals, Mr Barry's poems of da Pora in my pocket and the memory of Luke's recitation of the Principessa's poems in my mind that hot afternoon, it seemed that Italy was ablaze with the greatest poetry of Europe.

Certainly, the most noble of all Italian poets, both socially and intellectually, is the Principessa Nulana Nigonelli. Her family has kept vast wine estates in Campania for many generations, and has contributed greatly to military and Church life. In her childhood drawing-room at the Castello di Falanghina hang portraits of Generals and Cardinals who have left the Nigonelli mark upon armies and episcopal palaces throughout Italy. Her family has always been distinguished by that nervous and volatile sociability so peculiar to the nobles of the South. Her early childhood was one continuous round of visits and inspections.

ISCHIA

Ischia is your body
In the middle of a blue deep,
Limbs spread like the Bay of Naples
In the brine of sea-birds.

Earth-fresh wells are your temples,
Depth of blood, climax of honey—
You are the sea breeze to me
In my furnace of yearning;
You are the palliative
In fever.

It was on one such inspection to the family estates on the island of Ischia, a sojourn of many months in the company of her cousin, Count Marco Felluga, that she fell in love with a Venetian merchant trading out of Constantinople. She fell precipitously and with finality and, despite all the entreaties of her despairing cousin, sailed to the Eastern Mediterranean where she spent years of unbridled happiness, bearing her husband exquisite children and opening schools of design in silk and velvet. After many years she returned to Italy, encumbered by foreign manners and children who were at home in a different land. When she returned she carried with her a saddle adorned with jewels and an ingenious golden doll said to have been designed by the Venetian Ludovico Caorlino whose works were sold frequently in the golden markets of the Eastern Mediterranean. Even in her later years Venetian *tramoli* adorned her hair and Venetian clothing was yet her favourite indulgence. There is a portrait of the Principessa in a gown of scarlet *afigurado*, a dress of striking brocaded velvet by one of the master *velinderi* of the Lagoon.

The Principessa began to write her poetry in happy exile, encouraged no doubt by the educated merchants of Italy who lived at Constantinople. When she returned to Italy she did not return directly to her family estates, wishing to protect her children from the stress of their Christian blood relatives. She moved, instead, to the Court of the Queen of Naples. There her children were slowly prepared and strengthened for the social duties of adulthood, while the Principessa engaged in the arrangement of her poetry for publication. Her first volume of poems, published by I Libri Mercieri, a well-known bookseller of Urbino, caused a sensation throughout Italy. The Principessa avoided her new-found fame by engaging in the study of Antiquity. Encouraged in later years by the new Queen Maria Carolina, she took part in many archaeological excavations. She was with the Duke of Sussex, Sir Thomas Corbett and Mr Robert Fagan of Dublin when the famous Capitoline Venus was discovered at Laurentum. In 1797, by now in her mid-eighties, she shared with Mr Fagan in the discovery of the great Athena, a copy of the *Parthenos* of Pheidias, at Ostia. She persuaded Queen Maria Carolina to write letters of support for Mr Fagan who wished to search for Etruscan vases in Sicily. She travelled intermittently with Mr Fagan and his family. Five years after her death, Mr Fagan edited her extensive study, now lost, called *The Island of Sicily Reflecting Its Antiquities*.

But it is as poet that I wish to present the Principessa Nigonelli to the discriminating and educated among my own mercantile companions in Cork. It is now nearly fifty years since I first read her verse, twelve lyrics published in an exquisite calf-bound pamphlet. It was Luke Cleary who told me about her work, and Luke who has continued to inform me of her astonishing progress and fame. We had gone for our blessèd fortnight, our Irish *villeggiatura*, at Castel Gandolfo in the hills above Rome. Luke was particularly skittish and disturbed for he had been ordered to travel north to our house in Orleons where a group of French gentlemen loyal to the Church had expressed a wish to learn English from a clergyman with an Irish background.

It is to the eternal credit of the French that they interrogate the sources of all their knowledge, even the source of basic language skills. Luke's character had changed greatly in the year following his receipt of intelligence that his parents had purchased a four-hundred-acre farm south of Nenagh in County Tipperary. Such a level of propertied competence had accrued to his character that the Jesuit fathers took a much greater interest in him. At the time I felt that he would not be a mere Diocesan candidate for long, but would find himself shepherded into the grander citadel of the Society of Jesus. By this time, the 1760s and 1770s at Rome, much resentment was being expressed that the Jesuit Fathers were poaching the best priestly minds which had been destined for Ireland.

At that time Luke and I and Tim Delaney from Passage West worked seven hours in the vineyards and vegetable gardens. The fathers had planted carrots and cabbages and such conventional North European vegetables that Luke and I talked constantly of home. We talked, too, of the holy protector of the Irish race, Cardinal Ludovisi, who had bequeathed this cool patch of Italian soil to the devout Irish priesthood of Rome. It was then nearly one hundred and forty years since the holy Ludovisi died. I prayed quietly to myself as I worked in the fields, saying one hundred *Pater Nosters* and thirty *Ave Marias*. If we had an Irish Pope Ludovisi would surely be canonized. I was thinking too of Mrs Furnari. Her image came before my mind constantly as I thinned cabbages and restrained vines. She stalked my mind like a primitive huntress. It was then Luke Cleary told me of the astonishing connection between the Principessa Nigonelli and Cardinal Ludovisi. The Principessa was the Cardinal's great-great-grand-niece.

That evening Luke introduced me to the first published text of the Principessa. He had borrowed the book from the rector's private library. The little book of grey and gold calf binding had the smell of a young animal. Luke translated the Italian text 'Ischia'. We thought of the poem as a good sea-poem. We thought of the text as a kind of intense liturgy, something burning with clarity of desire and vision like the early Fathers in the desert. There is always something Biblical, certainly mythical, in the Principessa's poetry. Her thoughts have the fragrance of the East where she spent the most active portion of her young womanhood. But there was something else in the text, some intimate threat, that I found disturbing as a young man. The poem made me think of grapes in the vineyard that I had touched so gently, not wanting to disturb the bloom that is so crucial to the well-being of immature fruit. Expressions like 'depth of blood, climax of honey' seemed to belong to an untranslatable universe visible only to women. I was too young then to understand the series of unspoken female desires that under-lay all of the Principessa's work. It is a complex matter, but in the personae of her work the Principessa had unclothed Beatrice: it is Beatrice, beloved of Italian poetry, who desires to be the worshipper and not the god at the shrine of carnal love. At the core of the Principessa's work is that description of desperate, never fickle, human desire. Her work is infused with female passion, with that 'furnace of yearning'—certainly a new note in Italian poetry; and one that neither Luke Cleary nor I, twenty-year-old virgins, were equipped to discern. The texts had an erotic effect on us. To this day I can see Luke's lips moving as he held the book. He was praying for strength. Clearly God listened to him, as surely as God abandoned me, for Luke has had an extraordinary career in the life of the Church. I trace my downfall as a budding priest to that early discovery of the poems of Principessa Nigonelli. Through her implicitly carnal Class-icism I stumbled upon a series of phrases that explained my own carnal yearnings. Her texts were the bridge by which Mrs Furnari overwhelmed me.

FRATELLO

You, Santa Antonio
Or Heaven's Beloved,
Bound to the rocks
Of San Michele:
Your hands are full of skylarks.

You know me—
Bird of enticement.
Sometimes I am Eva,

Sometimes a venomous snake.
I rise in your mind
In the heat of a perfect day.

In 'Fratello' one can see how the Principessa has combined all those potent elements of womanliness, of temptress and Goddess. Words like 'bird of enticement' have all the purpose and potency of female passion, a passion both vulnerable and possessive. In these Kingdoms of Italy when a woman loves she risks more than the wreckage of feelings: she risks the complete loss of prestige and position. Until a woman is suitably betrothed she plays for terribly high stakes. The Principessa's abiding interest in Antiquity and Mythology courses through her poetic veins with the force of a fever on board ship. Reading the Classical authors and handling the lustreless shards and tiles of the past has given an added poignancy to the frailty of human feeling. Through History, her desires contain as many commands as yearnings, and her lines admonish the reader: 'To lie with thee / To give thee trial' may be read both ways; both as a direct and wanton offer of love and as a challenge to test a lover in the manner of a Professor examining a young scholar. The world that she has created in her poems is not an Italy that may lie in ruins, but a ruined world that may rise again in the arms of a powerful beloved. In this scholarship is as powerful as love, and a thing really loved has in a sense been truly studied.

Luke and I were truly overwhelmed by the force of the Principessa Nigonelli's voice. Nothing like it had spoken in the Italian world before. One thinks of the great Petrarch and Dante, and how each poet created a new Universe within which the Italian mind could live and grow, a Universe worthy of the colours and modes of life that came into the peninsula from the great Byzantine world of the East.

The Principessa, both captive, hostage, and yet of a Royal
house, has negotiated the terrible distances between the old
world of Superstition and Death and the new world of
Passion and Trade. Her poems embody that movement, that
uncertainty of love in a world under siege. In escaping and
writing she has found a new soul for the Italian tongue. 'She
has another poem here that I like,' I recall Luke's words as he
turned the pages of the pamphlet. 'It's about the times she
spent with a wealthy kinswoman south of Rome.' When
Luke had finished reading the poem he seemed disturbed and
unhappy, as if he resented its possession. It is true that as
seminarians we should not have been reading such uncen-
sored texts. We were straying into unknown territory, like
Christian captives in a pagan world. 'The Cardinal's niece,
she's a strange poet surely,' he said. 'We should pray for
her.' And we did. That day and many other days we prayed
for her and for her Ludovisi blood and name. In the poem
'In Settefratti' she has celebrated the place where her blood-
line began. It is a hymn to ancestors and a poem of praise to
the unrecorded poets of her family who remain, as ghosts of
making, at her side. Not only the family place, family
memory itself is the intimate enclosure where the scent of
poetry may be apprehended. The gift of poetry is like her
ancestral inheritance of golden hair.

IN SETTEFRATTI

In Settefratti
Is Castel Leoni,
Above Donna Livia's house.
From there the poet, Giovanni,
Out of Vesuvius,
Out of the hot cauldron,
Came with flame-coloured hair

And the flax of poems.
His poems fell to me
Through four generations.

In her poem she also celebrates the hidden recesses of her family estates, the flora and fauna, seasonal rhythms and hunts. She celebrates Italian woman as lover and herdswoman, as well as herbalist and huntress. She remembers well the summers she spent with noble kinswomen on estates at the very southern edge of the Bourbon Kingdoms. Enclosed within those images of childhood and early youth is that other image of the future, an image that propelled her into adulthood, the scene of the three ships of the Knights of Malta who came to spirit her back to the consolations of the Christian world. So one has that constant presence of an imagined elsewhere, even in her most sensual imagery; this elsewhere, it may be a future or a dream landscape, exists in each poem like a fine pastoral scene etched upon a handle of ivory or silver.

'Let us pray again, Nathaniel; these poems are too strong a thing for my mind,' I remember Luke's words. He blessed himself and I led our private session of prayer that allowed us to recover the ballast of Christ and His Church.

In those days, even as we prayed fervently, I could not banish my admiration for the work of poets. Poetry haunted me, not so much for its images or the special pleading it made on behalf of some poet's unanswered suffering, but because of its technical perfection over the passing world, the world of passions and trade. It began to dawn upon me, slowly but irreversibly, that a poem had a physical existence as weighty as a Freedom Box of Cork Corporation, but with more endurance. A poem was immortal. Even as I answered Luke's fervent *Ave Marias*, I knew that I had stumbled upon a great mystery.

97

I can never read the Principessa Nigonelli's lines now without Mr Barry's abrupt and immoral behaviour coming to mind. 'A luminous trout / Leaped from / The stream / To a woman's open bucket' seems a clear enough image to me, not requiring any licentious interpretations. Sometimes methinks that Mr Barry's mind was as clouded as the mixture of pigments upon his canvas.

In writing these great poems the Principessa has left us with a poetic tract on hope and hopelessness, and the victory of the virtues over all adversity. One can also see the moral anxiety of the Principessa in her admirable lyric 'Persephone', a poem of great spiritual depth and power:

> For I have been wicked, certain wicked,
> With an officer of your inner Corps;
> Riding side-saddle without
> Chaperone—
> But he was sweet-natured, as saturated
> With silk, as your own cicisbeo.
>
> He took me on wild rides
> Beyond the outer gates,
> His two colts so light of foot, so male
> With speed, you think the day had wings.

Here there is a metaphoric promise of the rescuing knight, a man of good breeding and even greater promises. This knight of the Principessa's poem is truly a man of the world, yet a creature of dreams who would distract a maiden to wander without chaperone, a dreadfully wanton act in the old Kingdoms of Italy. This poem, along with another forceful text, 'Thou', I have set for printing in later pages of this pamphlet. Both poems are linked by that common moral dilemma, the battle between desire and hope, between

dreams and virtues. I always think of the poem 'Thou' when
I think of that summer:

> *It is thou, unnamed cavalier,*
> *Who makes things real,*
> *Who has an ear for listening,*
> *I hope, to a Principessa*
> *With one story to tell,*
> *A Principessa barely escaped*
> *From the excesses of Constantinople.*

In this poem the Principessa has again addressed those twin
virtues: hope and fidelity. At the heart of every hope is a
rescuing 'Cavalier', a gay and promising metaphor surely,
and a good metaphor for every leap of faith and every
triumph over hopelessness in our lives. In each life we have
to face a series of trials, much like the tasks of ancient
chivalry in the stories of long ago. The Principessa has
shown that we may have to journey through life without
those verifiable trophies of success, whether those trophies
be the Venetian fortunes carried on board ship or the great
victory bonfires that were lit for the naval successes at
Lepanto. In creating these great works in the most trying
personal circumstances, the Principessa has built a single
epistle to the reader, a single interlocking text that must
continue to inspire the moral and political leaders of Italy.
From Bishop Luke Cleary's recent correspondence I am
reassured that all of these Principessa Nigonelli texts
continue to have a forceful and inspiring effect upon the
Italian world.

VI

THAT SAME SUMMER of the Principessa's poems was a summer of many mysterious happenings and events. There was a great deal of commotion in the streets of our *sestiere* because a baker who had prayed to the Sacro Bambino and climbed the steps on his knees to plead for the special favours of the Holy Child had won the Sacred Lottery. He celebrated his good fortune for nearly three weeks, drinking, dining, making festive noise—with all the neighbours and cousins that a simple man who strikes good fortune invariably attracts. He came to the College with a gift of five hundred zequines, nearly three hundred guineas, to be distributed among the priests of Ireland. He was of the impression that Ireland was a city and not a nation. The Rector did not disabuse him, but blessed him and thanked him in the name of Cardinal Ludovisi and other saintly Italians who had discovered within themselves a latent affection for our native land. Ireland's spiritual life will be forever indebted to those generous Italian impulses.

One evening I was called to the Rector's library for an interview. I wondered if a fellow-student had complained of Luke and myself reading uncensored texts. I knew that Luke had an undeclared copy of a Ravenna journal in his possession, and he had tried to make me promise that I should not lie if the Rector asked about its whereabouts. I told Luke that I could not betray him, thus putting a further nail in the coffin of obedience. However, the Rector had an extraordinary surprise in store for me. He had been invited to join the Furnari carriage at the *naumachia*, a carnival of water sports and a festival of light and music, to be held, as usual, in the Piazza Navona. Mrs Furnari had expressly wished that I would accompany the Rector to complete the Furnari suite. The Rector was not asking my opinion, nor offering a choice. He was issuing a command. He said that it was part of the duties of his leadership and his advocacy at Rome on behalf of the Irish Church that he had to participate in these tiresome social frivolities. 'Such things are a danger and a distraction to all of us,' he continued in a regretful tone, 'and far from the humble origins of the Divine Nazarene who was born in a stable. But we are all guests at Rome, Nathaniel, and guests of an impulsively generous and kind Kingdom. It is the good fortune of our Church that Rome is the place where Christ is interpreted for us, let us not forget that. There are other Kingdoms in Northern Europe where the Holy Spirit is interpreted in a bleak and colourless fashion. Let us give thanks to God for His Church.' Then he said the most unexpected thing. 'Your clothes, a new suit has been cut for you. I cannot have you looking like a Cork street urchin in the fine carriage of the Furnari.' He laughed.

That night of the *naumachia* comes back to haunt me now as I read the poems of the Principessa. I think of its sounds, its colours, and its hidden test of my deepest character and vocation. What a strange suite we made, an elegant couple and two priests, moving among the teeming revellers of the Roman night. We headed for what seemed an eternity aboard the Furnari carriage, a haven upon wheels that was brilliantly embellished and decorated with fabric and coloured timbers so that it looked like a Venetian gondola.

The Rector and I sat facing the Furnaris. Mr Furnari was a sickly gentleman who had the disconcerting tendency to stare at one long after one had spoken. I knew that he was a huge benefactor to the Irish College and had underwritten many clerical careers and journeys. It was said that he adored the Rector of the College, the Rector's love of his homeland and his high seriousness as well as his scholarship and undoubted appreciation of the decorative arts. The Rector, quite simply, thought Mr Furnari was a genius. Mrs Furnari spoke little, but seemed happy and animated by the loud noises of celebration. When we turned into the Piazza Navona we saw that the square had been ingeniously flooded so that a great sheet of water, like an inlet of the sea, lay before our eyes.

For nearly two hours we watched the water jousts and games, gondolas and flat-bottomed craft sailing by in a cacophony of music and colour. Every balcony and window was festooned with decoration. Sentries and policemen floated by, holding torches aloft, not to discourage the watery thieves but to add lustre to the scene. Gentlemen threw coins into the water and young children dived in to retrieve them. The Furnari coachman cracked his whip and roared, sending our lumbering carriage deeper into the water. I must have worn a worried expression for Mrs Furnari teased me for the first time that evening. She reassured me that the coachman knew every inch of depth beneath the horses' hooves. We wandered in a daze through the bustling water, speaking now and again only to point out some marvel of colour or illumination.

It was late in the festive evening when Mr Furnari invited the Rector to a *sabatine* in one of the nearby inns. The carriage turned and found purchase upon dry cobbles once more. We stepped down from our safe quarters and walked to an exquisite inn where tables had been laid out in the moonlight—only after twenty minutes or so did I understand that the moon itself was but an illumination in the night sky, an illusion manipulated from two aristocratic balconies by booms and pulleys. It was strange, that late into the night, for any youth to be abroad, never mind a priest in training, to dine upon pungent and expensive *vitella mongana* washed down by the rich wines of Montefiascone. The Rector saw me hesitate when wine was poured by Mr Furnari himself; but my dear mentor raised his hand in blessing. 'I absolve you this night, Nathaniel Murphy!' he said, blessing me. I made the sign of the Cross and drank. I recall my heady feelings after only minutes, the misted atmosphere of the carnival as it rotated around our table. I had more than three glasses of that lush and rich Montefiascone, enough to tilt the state of the entire universe for me: I was then not the portly creature of Penrose Quay, but light-bodied as a new-born calf. I could see the Rector and Mr Furnari deep in conversation, Mr Furnari being plied with more drink by the Rector, the two mature, even elderly men, at ease in each other's company. I recall Mrs Furnari speaking to me: about the priesthood, about Ireland and the great distances from Rome of countries beyond the Alps. She expressed the hope that I would remain at Rome and not return to the cold Northern climes of my boyhood. Sometimes we spoke in English, for Mrs Furnari, being the daughter of two famous noble families, the Gaetani and Ludovisi, had learned English from a Brighton governess. But I had fluent Italian and, even in an altered state of unreality, could reply in the language of our hosts. At that moment, instinctively and unconsciously, I would use Italian to distance my being from the effects of this woman. Mrs Furnari then engaged the Rector in conversation. The two elder men entered into quiet conference with her. I was the main topic of this conversation, but floated happily above the proceedings, not caring what the world might bring. That evening I was in a land beyond pain.

'You will accompany Mrs Furnari,' the Rector addressed me. 'You will be her Irish chaperone as she wishes to perambulate, to absorb the night.' With that he laughed, and Mr Furnari followed, also laughing. The very idea of this. To him, even in genial company, at this peculiar hour for a priest, an hour when only the viaticum bell should light the way of the ordained, it must have seemed bizarre, and without precedent in the life of a candidate for the priesthood. However, I think he was infected momentarily not only by the lush wines but by our unique distinction as guests of the Furnaris. It was our great honour, and in the manner of Italy he would do justice to that honour. I stood up immediately, obedient in public at least. 'Show her the colours of the night,' the Rector went on. Her husband nodded happily and she looked at me, smiling, expectant. I remember that look, penetrating and clear-eyed as if I was a child under scrutiny. I bowed to the company and turned to walk: I intended to clear her path. But I could hear the Rector's laughter behind my back. I turned round.

'Nathaniel,' he said, 'Please take Mrs Furnari's arm. It is night. You are her protector.'

I blushed, embarrassed by my lack of manners in such society.

'Mrs Furnari,' I said, offering my arm. She responded by linking with me in a most familiar manner.

We walked happily together, past the Furnari coachman who still awaited us at the edge of the watery *piazza*. The man bowed to his employer and they exchanged words. I thought for a moment that Mrs Furnari intended us to take to the carriage, but we passed on quickly into the crowded streets. There was a frantic happiness in the night air, music and illuminations, lamps whose reflection was caught now and again in the fine gold trimmings of Mrs Furnari's panniered red gown. Just then she seemed to me a most fantastical creature—most real in her physical presence, the raven black of her hair a perfect counterpoise to the red and gold of her clothes—yet, fantastical in the sense of her as a displaced presence in my priestly life. I was certain that no such creature had every walked the streets of Cork or wandered down the Mardyke of my native city in my youth.

'Look!' She pointed to the heavens. A great shower of light like a thousand falling stars illuminated the night sky. A cannon placed upon some battlement had released all of its compressed gunpowder. 'Oh. Beautiful. Beautiful,' she exclaimed as she traced the arcing orange and red lights as they expired into the darkness. I looked at her as she watched the night. Her perfect Italian face, sublimely well-bred, was like the face of a Madonna carved for some chapel of young Jesuits. She was the embodiment of perfection. Knowing that I was looking at her, she held her pose long after the stars of gunpowder had faded. She was well accustomed to admiration. We stood a long while as the crowds lunged forward, jostling, happy and inebriated. We listened to the music and stared at the many bizarre costumes; all theatrical garments of the night that I, lying a-bed in my College dormitory, could never have seen before. Mrs Furnari stared at me awhile and then, in a gesture of the most profound boldness, kissed me full upon the lips. Perhaps it was the shock of that moment or the wine in my blood, but I reacted as if her gesture was the most ordinary thing in Rome. I kissed her then in a manner that could only be licensed by betrothal. Her arms enveloped me at first, but then loosened and wandered about my person in a most inappropriate manner. 'Beautiful,' she whispered as she pushed her bosom against my chest. I need not describe in a book to be printed in my native city any further detail of that encounter. We stood alone, anonymous in the crowds of the Roman streets, the full weight of my priestly person against the body of this married woman; a woman distinguished in society and a comfort to many Convent committees and clergymen in need. The stiff fabric of the night was torn apart, my vocation lay upon the floor, tattered and useless.

'We should return to the table,' I said.

'Yes. Certainly.' She kissed me again and then broke away from me as if she were dispensing with an inappropriate gown. But when we walked she linked my arm again, seemingly content. She was a creature of convention. Convention and good manners, I was beginning to understand in my rustic naivety, form a single license through which much behaviour is forgotten and the most unconventional temporary activities are allowed. Yet there is another aspect to that evening that I can now see in hindsight and maturity. It is this: at that moment she had merely offered the first contract in a complex round of bargaining. Because I had responded at the level of desire I was now implicated in a new scheme of love that she had opened for herself. It was an unhappy place for a seminarian to be, though hardly a unique place in the Rome of those days. As far as her moral imagination was concerned, she was a married woman and therefore licensed for love, by Canon as well as Civil Law. It was I who was the thief and poacher, but that was of no concern to her. As man and foreigner I had complete responsibility for the destiny of my own immortal soul. Mrs Furnari, on the other hand, operated in that exquisite and splendid Kingdom of the forgiven flesh.

When we returned to the inn where we had dined the two older man had risen from the table. They were both looking down into the Piazza, watching the decorations and bunting being withdrawn from balconies to be stored yet again for the next Saturday night of revelry. Mr Furnari looked ill,

I thought, but he snapped into unexpected life when his wife ran to kiss him. They embraced each other as if they were the dearest friends in the world. At that time the accommodating mysteries of foreign marriage were beyond me. Mrs Furnari then turned to the Rector and kissed him with enthusiasm. Taken aback, he laughed with great kindness and touched her face with fatherly affection.

'Come, let us make haste,' said Mrs Furnari. 'Let us beat the dawn of Sunday or you will be late for your prayers! The old custodian will be horrified' (she referred to the strong-willed and iron-fisted native of the Trastevere who kept watch at the gates of the College each night).

'We cannot have that. Fabio would never allow us through the narrow gates!' the Rector joked. He staggered a little as he strained to adjust the ballast of too much wine.

'Let us go, then, my three men. I am too much a woman with such a richness of men.' She took her husband's arm and they walked together ahead of the Rector and myself in an atmosphere of complete happiness. I envied Mr Furnari his great luck: to share his life with such a splendid woman, to be overwhelmed each day by such fine breeding in his household. Yet he was a man of the world, a man of immense talent and wealth. It was a fair balance that such a woman was his counterpoise. For us men who carried within us a glimmering hope to serve the Church there was the consolation that we would serve the most beautiful woman of all, the Mother of God, Mary of Nazareth. Every Madonna in Rome, every grotto and painting, reminded us of that prayerful task at hand: to serve the Church and to reach Eternal Salvation through Him and through Her. When we had gained a footing upon the Furnari carriage and were moving noisily through the emptying streets I watched the Furnaris as husband and wife. They seemed fitted together, at ease, at peace with each other. I thought how lonely the priestly vocation; how one has to pray and adore forever without ever earning the favour of an embrace. Of course, such also is the immortal world of the greatest poets.

I was thinking thus of Mrs Furnari as I watched the distinguished couple in their carriage. Alone, she had an ungovernable nature; yet, with her husband she became most docile and tractable. Having been reared in Cork, in city trade and harbour commerce where caprice is never tolerated, the nature of such things was then a mystery to me. Travelling thus, sitting quietly by the Rector, I could observe their marriage with all the discretion of an English parson. The Furnari carriage made its way through a widening funnel of withdrawing crowds. We passed by a knot of singers at a street corner. They looked like the rustic minstrels who come at the end of each year from the Apennines to colour the streets and harvest the Christmas generosity of Romans. The tortured squeal of a bagpipe rose up to greet our carriage. Mrs Furnari ordered the coachman to halt. I could hear him grumbling. He hated the wintery noise, so out of place in mid-summer, and he wanted to hasten homeward as the crowds thinned.

But Mrs Furnari made to open the carriage door, the better to listen to the music. Just then the bagpipers ceased to play and a young woman, tall and wild-looking in her Apennine costume, began to sing. I was astonished. For what she sang was the text of the Principessa Nigonelli's poem, 'Venio ex Oriente.' She sang the poem with an indescribable depth of feeling. The crowd around her listened intently: 'There's henna in my hair / And pearls between my breasts', she sang with her chest filled and the rhythm rising ... 'The scents of honey bless / All my forbidden frills.' There was a magnificent resonance and depth to her voice: it carried the words of the great Nigonelli poem over the heads of all listeners so that the words seemed to leap at me and sit upon my lap.

'It's the Principessa Nigonelli's poem,' I said in astonishment. 'How extraordinary. It has already become a folksong in the Apennines.'

'Not the Principessa of captivity?' the Rector asked.

'You mean to say that is not a folksong?' Mrs Furnari suddenly addressed me, having ignored me completely since we had entered the carriage.

'Not at all. It was published at Ravenna nearly five years ago.'

'Truly. That is immortality,' the Rector observed. 'That is immortal, like the poems of our own dear Jacobites that are now the songs of the people. It is immortality of a kind, surely.' The Rector seemed deeply moved by the knowledge I had served to him.

The young countrywoman quickly moved to another song, this time accompanied by the woeful bagpipes. We waited a while, but as the coachman was now holding his impatience aloft for all to see, Mrs Furnari pulled the tassel of the door and it closed violently. The coachman mounted quickly. She struck the roof of the carriage with a little baton covered in purple velvet, a baton that had originally belonged, she told us, to her Ludovisi grandfather when he was Master of Ceremonies at some great function of the Papal troops. The Principessa's poem lingered. It was magnificent, a true reading and interpretation of a tremendous lyric, an embellishment of honour in such a talented voice. As a song it seemed not to require interpretation, and no one in the carriage at that moment seemed curious about its powerful intellectual qualities. I had already formed many opinions about the work; its perfection, its clear and musical lyricism as if the Principessa as she wrote it imagined some dancer or singer moving to its rhythm. It is, ultimately, a political lyric, with Jacobite codes from the nation of woman hidden within. These were not perceptions that could be shared with a company now exhausted from wine and food and the carnival of the night. Understanding this Principessa will take, methinks, time and the cooler scholarship of distance and translation.

I returned my suit of new clerical cloth to the Rector's office, knowing that it would be recycled at the first opportunity. I was not then of the opinion that it would be required again by me. The recovery of my soul, and the putting away of all worldly vanities, including the hidden journal out of Ravenna, was uppermost in my mind in the weeks that followed. I did have seven poems of Count da Pora, four printed in an Ancona broadside and three in manuscript, and these I tied into a bundle and hid away from my own insatiable need for poetry. One poem of the Principessa never left my sight, for I possessed it, word-perfect, in my memory: that was the lyric 'The Italian Question'. In the late Eighties of the last century I had that poem, along with Monsignor di Murthillo's 'A Trastevere Flautist', printed by Mr W. Flyn at the Shakespeare near the Exchange. We sold three hundred copies of the pamphlet on behalf of dear Fr Keating of the Brunswick Street Academy. The proceeds were used to offset the entrance guinea of many deserving youths of good family. Two famous men of Cork, the poet Fr English and the excellent old gentleman, Fr Arthur O'Leary, were associated with the school. They taught languages, English and the general *Belles Lettres*. It is appropriate that the sale of two such sublime Italian poems should have opened the gates of their instruction to more than a score of young Corkmen.

'The Italian Question' is as complete as a duck's egg, sitting perfectly upon the page even in its translated form, as perfect on the page as a boiled egg upon a linen napkin.

Yet its very perfection, its embodied music, is hugely decep-
tive. I have always considered it the most important political
poem of the Eighteenth Century. My friends in Cork, both
merchants and scholars, have considered my opinion hugely
inflated and hyperbolic. Yet no hyperbole could diminish
the achievement of this poem; it is hyperbole itself that
would need to come to terms with its majesty:

THE ITALIAN QUESTION

Hopeless, hopeless. I place in a boat, this,
All my hope, hope for Italian—
The way a mistress or mother might
Place in place a graceful infant

In a little vine-twisted, light ark
Of rush leaves, of rushes,
Its base made less feeble, thus,
With bitumen and, motherless,

Set this in a Triestine stream,
In familiar sedge
Or thick, thick rushes by the edge
Of some Adriatic; only

To have a graceful ebb and flow,
Ebbing, ebbing, not knowing
If the grace of such rescue might
Be a language, a daughter, an Italian.

It is said that menial talents in art worry greatly about
their status in the art world of the day, and that second-rate
poets fret constantly about their standing among the book-
sellers, but that great talents care about the survival of entire

worlds. For a poet the language itself is the world entirely. The Principessa Nulana Nigonelli, disturbed out of complacency by the trauma of early travel, was the first Italian to perceive a threat not to the little native world of poetic vanities, but to language itself. Her poem, therefore, is a desperate act of restoration; it is an attempt to rescue her language from the choppy harbour of invasions, the way a mother might attempt to rescue a child and bear it away to a place where it might live and be nurtured. In these days after the Empire, when the peace of Europe has been established and Italy has been restored to its patrimony, we cannot appreciate the urgency of threatened civilization that is contained within the Principessa's short lyric. There was a time when the very language of Italy itself was under threat. Hostile armies of occupation marched across the Lombard plains and the Veneto. Austrians sported at Urbino, the Spanish consumed Naples, and even the Russian empire had an efficient naval squadron and marines in the Adriatic and the Tyrrhenian Sea. We have forgotten these realities, the true context of this great poem. While the political urgency has passed away and the death of the Principessa's language will never happen now that Italy is free, the Irish reader would do well to contemplate the true force of poetry in its political context: that is 'the grace of such rescue' and 'All my hope, hope for Italian.'

The poet Giancarlo Oscharchigi, an officer of one of the Venetian regiments, is widely known and quoted in the Lombard Plains as well as at the ports of Genova and Livorno. It is hardly surprising that he is little known, and certainly under-rated, in his native Veneto, for poets are hardly ever recognized in their own native cities. Yet three exquisite editions of his work have been published by I Libri dei Friari of the Canereggio district in his native city, while an unusual orange-coloured card-bound quarto edition of his *Selected Poems* was printed at Torino in 1758. It is from the latter publication that I have made translations for my delight and education over many years. For over half a century Oscharchigi's poems have attached themselves to my most inner life. His is the work of love and adventure, with an attendant sense of great vulnerability and openness to the pain of life lost and lovers bereaved:

PORTRAIT OF THE CAPTAIN AS ARTIST

I am weary-dark with life in Castelfranco,
These officer-rooms in the Croce Barracks,
These narrow places that cramp my ambition.
My heart is turned to marble
In this quarter of drunken alms.
In place of hammered poems
I am speechless among the improvisatori.

While still a very young officer he fought many battles in that difficult mountainous terrain of the Austrian borders. His constant companion during these campaigns was a young subaltern of a noble house of Firenze. When I first met the Captain—it was at Lucca, on my own final journey out of Italy—he showed me a miniature oil of this young subaltern, a dark-haired youth with the blazing eyes of his mysterious Hellenic mother. Il Capitano Oscharchigi is uncommonly attached to the memory of this beautiful youth who died of a fever after coming ashore at Mestre: his poetry is saturated with images of this young man, or, more accurately, with absences that can only be interpreted as the absence of a beloved. The loss of his young companion endures as a kind of grey muslin of grief stretched over the fretwork of poetry. Even a poem as straightforward as 'Portrait of the Captain as Artist' lives in a clear co-existence with death. 'It is pain / Beyond endurance, this Veneto silence' is a heartfelt expression of grief, an imaginative flattening of the architecture of Venice into a memorial silhouette rather than a coloured landscape. It is poetic thoughts only that may burst into flames, yet thoughts barely warm enough to dispel the cold fog of 'gossip'.

We may think of the disturbances of our own nation, the idealistic Patriot activities of the United Irishmen and the more recent rebellion of poor Emmett in Dublin, and wonder at the lack of deep genius that our own land has produced in recent times. Compared to the rebellious and patriotic poets of Italy our own poets have been remarkably silent of late. We have nothing to show for that forest of pikes at Wexford, the bloody embarrassment of thirty years, but a few street ballads and a number of ill-considered political pamphlets. It is a cause of national shame that in a time of great energy and sublime revolt in English poetry, Ireland has produced no poet of genius. Further, it is remarkable that the exclusive love of Ireland has produced no great work of literature. Those writers among us who have produced fine literature have been attached, however loosely, to England and England's distinctive civilization. I am not qualified to speak of our native Irish language. Indeed, that language may hold poets of brilliance, but they are alien to the commerce of our cities and cannot contribute to the discourse that alters life in the present century. When I think of the physical bravery and amorous sensitivity of Giancarlo Oscharchigi and contrast such depth of humanity with the common horde of Irish writers I am driven to despair. In the poem 'Here at Palazzo Balbi' our glorious Captain of the North catalogues with affection the squares and quays of his native place:

Here at Palazzo Balbi
I name my hidden islands,
My Ponte, my Rio, my Canal.
Here, I am at one tide-level
With every outlook, each lagoon.
Here I understand
The permanence of water
As I gauge each sestiere,
The great loop of the Canale Grande
Where every Lombard settled
For a thousand years.
Here, opened before my eyes,
From Palazzo Grimani
To the Ca' Rezzonica,
Is the Palazzo of my people,
Is the Murano glass of water.

Born in a great trading city he understands 'the permanence of water' and that 'flotilla of pride' so commonly understood by those who are born in that buoyant cradle of a busy trading city. He has lived in that place where business gets done, where all men live by that common 'statute book of the sea'. In every way, Il Capitano Oscharchigi's work belongs to those final days of my priestly life in Italy. I never associate his work or his spirit with my sojourn in Rome, but, rather, with a life of flight and anxiety as I tried to find a way back to my homeland. Only quite recently have I confided the details of my last weeks in Italy to my colleagues in business and at the Athenaeum. Indeed, Alderman Wrixon and Dr Penrose have been adamant that I include the final circumstances of my flight from a dangerous Europe in any explication of my Italian poets. I am a mere translator, it is true, but the circumstances of how a translator escapes with his texts are always of interest to a scrutinizing intelligence.

VII

It was at Lucca, on my flight to the coast and the safety of Livorno, or Leghorn, that I first came across the poems of Oscharchigi. The circumstances of my flight from Rome seem bizarre and improbable now. But I found myself the victim of strange circumstances. It is not necessary to call everything to memory, but my oldest friends have persuaded me to set down the facts. I have never had the power to thwart the enquiring inclinations of my best companions in Cork. Even the highest ranking Corkman is an insatiable gossip, ever willing to risk reputation and peace of mind in pursuit of some prurient intelligence. It is our pursuit of gossip in this haven royal that has led to much argument and dispute: dispute and argument are such parasites of energy, such enemies of a truly creative life. In our own lifetimes at Cork we have seen such humiliating circumstances, instances where men of the most subtle genius dedicate their waking hours to the pursuit of some pitiful personal vengeance. Such lives of revenge, of heated, pitiful quarrel, cause poets and men of business to look ridiculous as they grow older; and cause entire family names to become still more degraded objects of posthumous ridicule.

It was my destiny to experience strange things, even to suffer wickedness, when I lived far away from Cork, far distant from the steadying ballast of Family and City. Oscharchigi's poems are among the pearls that I have dragged to the surface from the depths of elsewhere. In keeping with my friends' advice and my friends' undoubted sense of mischief, I have kept to the facts of these poems. I have remained faithful to the tone of the earthy Italian. I hope I shall never take the unbecoming freedom of censuring persons of such heavenly character as Count da Pora or the Principessa Nulana Nigonelli or Il Capitano Oscharchigi. Their names are not known at all in the Kingdoms of Britain and Ireland. When I study their work in the original language I recall the electrifying effects of their first publication. I am made aware quite how unfit I am to be their translator. But destiny, and destiny alone, has caused me to be their first prolocutor in this our safe haven on the cold North Atlantic. 'Here, opened before my eyes, / From Palazzo Grimani / To the Ca' Rezzonica, / Is the Palazzo of my people' writes the incomparable Oscharchigi, adding to his faithfulness a great litany of quaysides. His works reminds me—as I have warned my friends in the Cork Library—that their real fame in Britain must await a sharper pen than mine, a more passionate Mediterranean mind. Dr Johnson himself has warned us: 'The grand object of all travelling is to see the shores of the Mediterranean. On these shores were the four great Empires of the world; the Assyrian, the Persian, the Grecian and the Roman. All our religion, almost all our law, almost all our arts, almost all that sets us above savages, has come to us from the shores of the Mediterranean.'

I do recall with complete clarity and distaste the beginning of my end at Rome. I remember an evening, not many weeks after our night in the Furnari carriage, a little after the *Ave Maria* bell had sounded, when the Rector came to me at my private prayers to ask yet another favour. He asked if I would accompany Colonel Ottoboni, a distant relative of the Cardinal of that name, to the Tuesday *conversazione di prima sera* at the Furnari residence. There was no question of refusal. I was made ready in the usual manner, toileted and clothed to seem like a clerical gentleman, a cleric above my station. The Colonel and I arrived late at the residence: servants were already moving about with a second round of ices and biscuits. The Furnaris were thrilled of course to greet the Colonel, knowing well his Church connections. They all embraced like long-lost friends. After Mrs Furnari had embraced the Colonel she turned to me and took both of my hands. 'Ah, Nathaniel. Oh! Such cold hands in one so young! See, feel them.' She placed her husband's warm hand over mine and feeling them I suddenly became aware how cold I must seem to others. 'Here, Nathaniel,' she said gently. She picked from a marquetry side-board a silver flask wrapped in blue linen. 'Here. The *cassetina* will warm you.' I took the warm bundle and felt the heat. She seemed happy to watch me warming my hands. Mr Furnari and the Colonel turned away from us almost immediately. They recognized an elderly man who occupied one of the few chairs in the room. 'A banker,' Mrs Furnari said, amused. 'Everyone has to pay homage to old Aldobrandi.'

The men, priests, Cardinals, bankers, moved together and created a kind of private society like sea captains in the coffee-houses of Castle Street and Nile Street in Cork. Mrs Furnari was left to attend to me, a deacon of no property in the world of Rome. 'Come, you must see our apartments. You never get to see the world, Nathaniel.' She took my arm as casually as the night of the *naumachia* and we paraded through a file of exotic persons in the finest cloth I had ever seen in my life. We moved through a room full of music where everyone seemed inebriated by the ices served, through a passage that was hung with severe oils of the Holy Family set in the most elaborate Baroque frames, into yet another room where a small fire blazed in a fireplace of Carrara marble. There a Cardinal of the church and two young women were laughing uproariously. Disconnected from the Colonel, I was languid with curiosity and feasted upon the sight of such noble company, the bankers and the minor nobility of Rome. Eventually we reached Mrs Furnari's private apartment, a kind of high-ceilinged sewing chamber that was festooned with silks and velvets, woollens and feathers, leathers and gilt buckles, all hanging in a chaotic pattern from frames and chairs and contraptions of wood and brass that protruded from the walls. Mrs Furnari moved to adjust the wick of an oil lamp; the room became softly illuminated as the wick rose. Mrs Furnari's face glowed with a kind of almond beauty. She took my hand and whispered in a throaty Trastevere accent; an unexpected vulgarity in such a noble setting. She placed my hand upon her warm neck. 'You are warm now, dear Nathaniel. Prince of Ireland!'

'I am not a Prince,' I said proudly, mustering that fierce resistance to kings that we pride ourselves upon in Ireland. 'My family are but common merchants.'

'No! A Prince from the North. You are the Prince of merchants! My husband says you have the grace of royal blood. Will you comfort me, *principe*?' She kissed me then with great hunger, and as she did so I could feel the agitation of her knuckles against my chest: she was loosening her bodice. Deftly she made herself half-naked, and my hands, full of the *cassetina*'s warmth, moved over her with an unpriestly abandon. In these years of my maturity when old age has filled my passions with manners and restraint, it is difficult to describe the abandonment and urgency of my twentieth year. What a harrowing thing celibacy is; what a coiled spring, and what overwhelming grace of God must be available to restrain a young man's passion when it is offered a conduit half-clothed in Italian silk. At that moment in the Furnari apartment all of God's grace abandoned me. I had fallen: as a moral being, a priest promised to Rome, I was now completely compromised. But my youthful hunger did fall upon that married woman, voluptuous, beautiful, grossly irresponsible—a divine spirit clothed with the miraculous glow of a body fed upon olives, sturgeon, venison and the first ripe cherries of the Naples valley. We stood, or lay, rather, against an almost mystical mound of expensive cloths. We were partly clothed and working ourselves to pleasant exhaustion. I do recall that moment as a kind of boyish triumph, a moment of supreme pleasure untempered by the stress of business and marriage. Mine was a poacher's pleasure, devoid of any sense of husbandry or ownership. Mrs Furnari seemed perfectly unperturbed and happy. Only later, in our own devoted maturity, could I begin to understand these things. My beloved Louise has many theories on the relationship between men and women, theories that she has applied to my situation as an untried youth in a strange land. My Louise in her wisdom says that I was trapped by a marauding voluptuary: ours was the kind of moment for which Mrs Furnari hunted in the relaxed, licensed world of the Rome of long ago. I do recall with satisfaction my youthful weight upon those exquisite curves and mounds. Indeed I felt like a prince: I am sure that I was neither the first nor the last of her extramarital conquests. We were suspended for what seemed like an eternity in a world of cloth and yellow lamplight. Voices and footsteps sounded in the corridors; laughter too, and distant music. Mrs Furnari considered them all with pleasure. I whispered, 'Mrs Furnari, we should return to the society of the rooms. Colonel Ottoboni will be searching for me.'

'Camilla', she whispered. 'Say it. Camilla. My mother's name.'

'Camilla.' I whispered her name as instructed. And repeated it until she began to smile. I thought of her name as an accusation, but she smiled at my Irish accent that made the Italian sing even more. She turned from me, then, to compose herself for the world beyond the cupboard. Seeing her thus, I pulled her playfully to me and distracted her for my own pleasure. I was not merely negligent, but sinning. 'Truly,' she said, kissing me, 'you were not born for the Church.' We were suspended for a moment in that cocoon peculiar to the very young; transfixed, and not at all suitable companions for the world of conversation. In Mrs Furnari's arms I felt no 'prince of tears, no prince of thorns' as the sublime Oscharchigi says in his 'Veneto Sanctuary'. In his poem Oscharchigi writes with reverence of the foothills of the Veneto, 'Down the mossy aisle, a carpet / Among the tufted pews', reminding each reader of the heavenly solace of contemplation and the refuge of wilderness. In one sense love is the best refuge for the human soul, it is the height gained and the dry cave discovered. Part of Il Capitano Oscharchigi's power is that very real sense of the soul at rest, looking outward at life, judging and remembering in isolation. 'With the breath of life not the breeze of grammar, / The God of Italy shows His face' is how the poet instructs us to live our lives. At that moment in Rome I had certainly chosen too much of the breath of life, and too little of the grammar of Mater Ecclesia. But the stress of love and love's bitter and eternal demands are powerfully captured in his masterful 'Piccadelio: Nightfall'. Here the poet-soldier languishes in a kind of after-world of love and soldiering, in an ante-chamber of despair:

> *I am frantic in the aftermath*
> *Of waiting. Some friend.*
> *Here at the heart of Piccadelio,*

At the channel mouth
Of undertow, the barbed wind
Of the lagoon shreds my bones,
The Ottoman of hunger
Stains my tunic, hordes
Of destruction skin me alive,
And you, you gondolier
Of a thousand kisses:
The tide of you goes out.
If I went begging for alms
Or fell on my two knees
Right here in the marina of sighs
Would some lion-hearted boatman
Step ashore benignly
From the flotilla of the vain,
The deceitful of the Doge
Who pole a wide berth from me
As if I were a cargo
Of cholera.

'The tide of you goes out', he says, creating thus a supreme metaphor of love lost.

Few who have lost in love have been able to plot the course of retreat so completely. Waiting and agitation, yearning and loneliness, all have a place in the catalogue of Oscharchigi's poems. No poet of my Irish homeland has been able to create such a map of love's afterlife; that glow of hopelessness before the lamp is extinguished:

An angel of Fuseli
Walks the canvas of night,
Swallows flying
In the suck-suck of her boots;
But like the Ace of Hearts

In a Venetian Tarot pack
She slips away.
A hunchback castrato
Sings on a sheltered quay
In Lower Piazza Santa Maria,
The prophetic cry of his hymn
Like the snagged whimper
Of a boatman's spaniel.

Would that Irish poetry had the philosophical strength of Italy. I well remember reading these poems for the first time while I waited nervously on the white-hot ramparts at Lucca. But I anticipate my narrative—that was eight days into our flight from Rome. From Lucca we had taken the road westward to Livorno where we would seek passage to Marseilles. But, again, I anticipate. Poetry forces upon us such jumps in attention, such an upstart of narrative. It was from Mrs Furnari's hands (retreating from the greatest act of foolishness in her life) that I received the card-bound quarto of Il Capitano's poems. I treasured them for many years until the arrangement of my marriage and the birth of our children put everything belonging to the past into a grey perspective. The past loses its intensity and essence as one watches one's children grow and business develop. Truly, for a man happily settled into the task of a life of business and enterprise in the port of Cork, the past becomes but a shadow, a minor thing. What vivifies and gilds the past for me are the emotions released by these Italian poets. The scent of Italy is still upon them. Yet, the memory of that apartment in Rome, the silks and the music, does 'step ashore benignly' as Oscharchigi has written.

That evening Mrs Furnari composed herself for the corridors and the society of her husband. We both emerged from that sewing-room as lightly and adroitly as unlicensed lovers could. No one seemed to notice our restoration to the lights and pictures and pockets of gossiping clerics and society women. We moved gingerly back through the room with the marble fireplace: the young women had now disappeared but even more Cardinals and Monsignors, languid and melancholy, attended to the dying fire, speaking loudly and musically of the destinies of ambitious Romans. I searched the rooms anxiously for Colonel Ottoboni, but couldn't find him among the seated or the standing who were still gluttonously consuming the last of the Furnari ices. 'Camilla!' a voice called from behind us both and we both stopped abruptly and turned. It was Mr Furnari. The Colonel stood beside him, a little inebriated, head bowed as if he was inspecting his shoes. 'Have you given Fr Nathaniel the correspondence from Count da Pora?' he asked. 'It came to us from Mr Barry through my sister-in-law,' he addressed me in a friendly manner that immediately put me at ease. 'Yes, yes. I forgot. Let me get those letters.' Mrs Furnari fussed with her hair, ill at ease.

She walked back along the corridors and opened the door to a compartment beyond the sewing-room. She disappeared inside, then reappeared quickly carrying a bundle tied together with a black ribbon. 'A letter and three poems,' she said. 'Mr Barry said that Count da Pora has fled from his apartments at Ancona. There has been no word of him since this letter. Mr Barry wants you to have this correspondence.' She handed over the package—not to me but to her husband, who, in a gesture of unannounced formality took one step back, bowed and handed the package to me. 'For you, Fr Nathaniel,' he said, 'for you to preserve and keep, for you to carry back to the island of Ireland; for you to translate and publish in your native city. The patrimony of Le Marche must be preserved.' He turned to his wife. 'Is that not true?' he asked. 'Were those not Mr Barry's words as reported by your sister.' Camilla nodded her head. 'Yes. Those were my sister's words.' With that transfer of the precious documents the business of the evening seemed to have concluded. The Colonel said that he should leave and the Furnaris understood. He was a man of important connections and theirs was only the first, therefore the least prestigious, of his *conversazione* of that night.

The Colonel and I exited quickly and made our way by efficient coach back to the gates of the Irish College. There I was summarily ejected, along with the valuable package, while old Ottoboni continued on to his next social engagement. I never quite understood why I was asked to accompany the Colonel, a man of superior station in life, to the Furnari family. I wondered if he was in league with the errant wife; if he wasn't an agent of her illicit loves who found therein a vicarious pleasure. When I had gained the privacy of my own cubicle I read the letter of Count da Pora and the sublime poems. What an astonishing privilege it was for me to have personal possession of such mementoes. The Count's letter was full of desperate intrigues and seditious politics. Things were at a bad state in Ancona. Now I think of the words of Il Capitano Oscharchigi rather than the words of da Pora: 'O God of Ironies, / Such a saving intervention.' No such interventions were available to Count da Pora at that moment in Le Marche.

The works of both Italian poets dominate my mind now as I remember. Their distress in Italy was much more real than mine, and full of potential danger. The pain of moral and political life communicated in their brilliant verses is the kind of pain with which I could have instant fellowship that night in my Irish College. Their work reminded me of the tragedy of this life, a vale of tears when we begin and a valley of death when we end. Even now, I am aware of the too intimate details of my personal youth in these pages, such material for censure within. I am aware that a man is never so decidedly condemned as on his own confession. But the words of these poets whom I have translated, in all humility, are inextricably linked to the circumstances of my youth at Rome. Indeed, without the work of these poets I feel my youth has no valid and verifiable memory. As I remarked to Mr Penrose in a recent conversation, without them my present soul has no background. I was a foolish young deacon with an entirely separate mental world already formed from the reading of just a score of these poems. I would beg the present reader to bear with these memories in a spirit of private trust: if the truth be told, life at the end will find each one of us condemned.

A few days afterward I received a letter from home; this time in my mother's hand-writing. The letter was full of the more innocent and familiar gossip of Cork, but also contained a most damning piece of intelligence. There had been a serious business failure, something to do with wagers between my cousin and several rakes at the Mallow Spa. The family was suddenly of questionable solvency. It was a matter of great urgency and distress at home. Our good name was questioned. My father, always one of the most loved and respected Catholic merchants of Cork, had been excluded from a meeting of the Committee of Merchants at Ruggs Tavern. My mother's distress was palpable. I could see that her letter was written in tears. In the night isolation of my cubicle, pressed to grief by the alternating rage of Count da Pora and the grief of my poor mother, I knelt to the floor and prayed fervently. I prayed to God in Heaven and his Holy Mother to alter circumstances, to send me home, failed, humiliated but intact of body, to speed me homeward upon some magic coach of prayer. At that moment I missed the companionship of Luke Cleary who had moved on a six-month mission to our house in Orleons.

Luke was my Giuseppetto, the Colonel of like but steady mind who would advise and give good counsel to me in the manner of Il Capitano Oscharchigi's superior officer.

Oscharchigi's superb poetry of waiting—of a life suspended between a parish of personal failure and a destiny of exile—best expresses how I felt at that moment in my Irish College. My youth in ruins, my family in ruins, I could hear the prophetic cry of the *castrati*, the whimper of a whipped spaniel, and the future like a ghostly apparition painted for me alone by some ambitious Geneva lunatic. Later, I felt that I too had been visited by the Venetian harlot but, unlike Il Capitano, I had been found morally wanting. In 'Piccadelio: Nightfall' Oscharchigi has charted a superb journey along a narrow and compromised route of personal ruins. Few poets of Italy have achieved that kind of committed personal depth, depth of personal soul alone, that is; of the soul as it makes its betrayed journey towards a new kingdom of salvation. I recall my later journey on a coaster out of Livorno, reading these poems for their comfort in a rough sea. This poem was committed to memory by the time we reached the port of Marseilles. In youth life jests with our immortal soul. Inappropriate opportunities occur, moments of ill-advised opportunity like the presence of an Ace of Hearts in the cards of the Tarot cult. With blood racing in his veins, every young man calculates, seizes the opportunities of the flesh without counting any of the political consequences of love. Oscharchigi loved deeply and hopelessly, isolated from opportunity in the uniform of an officer at barracks, offering to his beloved but the 'snagged whimper / Of a boatman's spaniel.' After Petrarch, surely, he is the great Italian poet of love.

VIII

DAY FOLLOWED DAY in bleakness as I thought of the troubles in our family business in Cork. The Rector of our Irish College, always a most kindly, holy and sophisticated man, having dutifully censored my letters and become alerted to the complications of my soul, interviewed me at length on five afternoons of the following two weeks. A second letter had arrived for me, in my father's hand, outlining the misfortunes of the Murphy enterprise. My first cousin, Bartholomew Boylan, had sworn ownership of the family enterprises while gambling with three gentlemen, one Kingston, one Bowen and one Arbuthnott, at a Mallow tavern and brothel. He had mortgaged the business in an effort to buy time while gambling; all gamblers are like drowning sailors who snatch at anything that floats in order to purchase buoyancy. It was our misfortune that cousin Boylan snatched the one buoyant thing at hand, the family enterprise. He was my father's partner, with full authority to risk assets. The three Cork gentlemen, being gentlemen of the Ascendancy, proceeded to claim their pounds of flesh. My father stated in his letter that all contracts, cargoes and auction rights had been lost. One warehouse at Nile Street and an interest in a lime kiln at the top of Spring Lane had been saved by auctioning twelve rare pink shells that had

129

been a gift to my father in boyhood from a former ship's Commander of the East India Company. At auction in Dublin the rare shells had realized eight hundred guineas. Part of the patrimony of my father's life, they were among my mother's most prized possessions. My father wrote that their loss was a greater pain than all of the lost merchandise and goodwill in Cork.

But misfortune visits us in squadrons. One day I was again reading both letters, comparing my mother's and my father's handwriting—my mother so orderly and distinctive, my father so heavily inked and functional—when yet another great and malevolent event occurred in my priestly life. I heard a thunderous and ungentlemanly rapping upon the door of our dormitory. Peeping through the curtain of my cubicle I saw three military-looking men in heavy boots make haste towards me. I checked my buttons and stood at attention to receive them. I heard the Rector's voice behind them, his pleading, and a tone of panic so unexpected in our safe College environment. 'This is a mistake,' he was pleading. 'This is truly ridiculous.'

The three military police stood beside me, as if they formed a guard of honour or were part of a squadron of Papal courtiers. Then the sergeant addressed me. 'Dottore Murphy, we wish to search your apartment, under authority of the Cardinal. You have been reported.'

'Deacon,' I corrected him, for I was not in the least fearful. So many strange things had happened to me by this time that I accepted without alarm every dramatic occurrence. Rendered senseless to the realities of the world by a cascade of bad news, I felt that I was living among actors in a colourful but macabre theatre.

'Under authority of the Cardinal we must search your apartment for seditious documents. Prepare yourself to accompany us.'

The Rector remonstrated with the sergeant: 'No! No! This is a terrible mistake. Nathaniel is one of our dearest, dearest young priests. He is of good family. Good and important Catholic family in Ireland,' he lied. 'There will be serious repercussions for us, I tell you! His family is a great ally of the Church.'

'Stand aside, *Dottore*,' the sergeant addressed him. 'We have intelligence of his seditious connections. Please stand aside.'

One of the military officers stood back, as if to keep the entire company under surveillance, while his two colleagues began their search. They were methodical and respectful, and continuously under the hawk-like gaze of the Rector. He placed his hand upon my shoulder in a fatherly gesture of affection and shook his head. I reassured him, for I was not then in the least anxious for my own position. As I have written, their intrusive presence was but one more bizarre incident in a catalogue of unreality. The two men soon fell upon the correspondence of Count da Pora. They conferred with the third member of the group and he stepped forward and addressed me most severely: 'You will come with us,' he said. 'These matters require a fuller cooperation from you.' At these words the Rector completely lost self-control. He shouted at the senior member of the force, insisting yet again that I was of good family, devout follower of the Church, a most loyal student who had travelled great distances for my religion. The idea that I was involved in any kind of seditious activities was a great calumny. But these members of the State security were men of stern and unbendable will. All was lost. As Il Capitano Oscharchigi has written, 'In the pure coldness of my mind / I recognize the true absence of a friend.' Mindful indeed of 'the Christ tempted in the desert' I kept my composure and did not offer resistance. One of the many lessons in life that I had already learned from my father was that a man must not add fuel to the fires of disturbance. Most violent acts, of aggression and resistance, occur when the bile is up and tempers have risen—with police and military, as with all members of the public service, it is best not to antagonize. When tempers are risen, my father always said, neither business nor art can be concluded. I accepted my arrest with the same passivity with which I had greeted Mrs Furnari's immoral approaches. The Rector, still shouting, demanded to see a document, a warrant of authority. The senior member of the group pulled the necessary warrants from his coat. The Rector examined them. I could see his face growing pale with the reality of the situation: these men acted with the full authority of a Cardinal.

I was soon bundled into a carriage reserved for criminals of the diplomatic corps. It was only then I realized that a mistake of dreadful proportion had taken place. A mere deacon, I could never merit a carriage such as the one that now lumbered through the Roman streets. Several people bowed to me as I passed by, seeing me as a personage both exalted and doomed. I carried only my breviary and crucifix, and a little silver canister of Holy Water that was embossed with the crest of the City of Cork. It had been a gift to my mother from the merchant house of Hickey and de Souza of Lisbon. Upon arrival at the military barracks I was immediately placed in a cell with three other wretches; one a brilliant and humorous Sicilian smuggler of pearls, the other two mere forgers employed by the British Ambassador. The two British forgers and I struck up a great friendship, as nearly always happens when Irish and English gentlemen meet abroad. The two had been caught red-handed in the Quirinal while copying a Papal license to trade with Church estates in Chile and Peru: the forged document had been a special request from the Admiralty.

They were both awaiting release upon payment of substantial fines by our Government. When I read of the great wealth of Italy, the lustre of the Veneto in Oscharchigi's poem—'the luminous silk / Vulgar gold, of La Fenice'—I contrast it all with the reality of a cobbled dungeon, the drab reality of my twelve days in that Roman prison. I am certain that the Rector tried to communicate with me, but I received no inkling of his interest or efforts on my behalf. The English forgers, who seemed to have an endless supply of Roman currency, kept both the Sicilian pearl-fisher and myself in bread and wine. I was twice taken into a private apartment for interview, interrogated at length by persons who seemed to be from Poland or the Austrian territories. They certainly grew bored with my company, for I knew nothing of seditious activities in Ancona or anywhere on the Adriatic coast. I did speak with passion of Count da Pora's poetry. At one point, having finished reciting one of the Count's finest poems, I was struck on the face by an exasperated clerical inquisitor. I was shocked by such violence towards an Irishman, and such unwarranted violence from a subject of some worthless empire beyond the Alps.

Though weakened and disoriented by my imprisonment, I was still buoyed up by that insolence and self-importance that is such a treasure and friend of youth. When I returned to my cell after that impromptu beating I was treated with great tenderness by the English forgers. Indeed, their sympathy and kindness led to an embarrassing encounter on the night following my beating. Driven to pity by the blackness of my eye and the swelling around my nose, they arranged for the visit of a woman of the night, an agreeable and very drunk young woman who exposed herself without shame before my eyes. I feasted upon that fruit of the world, but prayed to Heaven for strength. It was only when I started to weep, following her heavily exaggerated demonstrations of affection and interest, that the two Englishmen kindly redirected her attention to the Sicilian fisherman who, in due course, and in full view of the other men in the cell, claimed his Trastevere pearl. I prayed heartily through the jeers and ribald laughter of the cells.

On the twelfth day of my illegal imprisonment two well-dressed English-speaking gentlemen arrived at our cell and engaged the Admiralty forgers in animated conversation. They distributed coins among the obsequious warders, who bobbed and bowed with such fervent hypocrisy that one of the gentlemen, speaking fluent Italian, warned them to remove themselves from the company or they should not see the balance of payment due to them. Needless to say, they fled. In every civilization the promise of immediate payment brings results. Then they turned to me and introduced themselves. They were both clerics of the Protestant faith, informal agents of the Crown. They introduced themselves as the Rev. John Hobhouse of the Anglican communion and Rev. Dr Charles Dalkieth of the dissenting Church of Scotland; an unusual companionship at that time, for the Dissenters of Scotland were then as despised and abandoned in the Kingdoms as our own Catholic faith. I was not surprised to learn that it was a common friendship with Mr Edmund Burke that had brought them together to Mr Barry's studio to inquire into the circumstances of the great painter's life. There, they had found Mr Barry agitated by my disappearance, and made ill by the knowledge that his enthusiastic transfer of Count da Pora's papers to my safe-keeping had been the undoing of me in the eyes of an ill-advised police force. I was fully to blame for the loss of my vocation to the priesthood, but Mr Barry's seditious poet friends were certainly an instrument of that undoing.

I did not return to our Irish College upon my release into the semi-darkness of the Roman evening. Nor did I attempt to show myself at Mr Barry's studio, for the Rev. Hobhouse warned me that the police kept it under surveillance. This piece of intelligence depressed me deeply. But I was shepherded away by a friend of the two clergymen and deposited safely into the studio of a group of agreeable English artists who lived near the Palazzo Piombino on the Strada del Babuino. They were welcoming, yet utterly uninterested in my situation. It was there I met Robert Home, the well-loved Dublin portrait painter who in later years became as famous for his beautiful wife as for his art. After several days I was moved to a house in the parish of San Lorenzo, and then to a quiet and beautiful house on the Strada Felice in the parish of Sant'Andrea delle Fratte. I knew I could never again see the dear Rector of our Irish College, for in the Rome of those days to be accused was to be guilty. I would not endanger the well-being of the College by too close a contact with it. I wondered if I should ever again see the great genius, Mr Barry.

Imagine my surprise when, on the fourth day of my peripatetic existence, Mr Barry himself and a gentleman, Pietro Ferri, who was an employee and close confidant of Cardinal Rezzonico, arrived at my hiding place. They carried all my papers, letters and personal effects from the Irish College, including a letter from the Rector that contained enough money for my journey home to Ireland. The sight of the Rector's handwriting made me weep. Mr Barry began to weep also, mumbling the names of his brothers who, he cried, were all now dead in Cork. I think of Il Capitano Oscharchigi's words when I remember those moments: 'Lagoon of suicide, / Towers of madness' and that wonderful line: 'It is difficult to master gloom.' I composed myself quickly, but Mr Barry wept again when he handed me the correspondence and poems of Count Luigi da Pora.

The Cardinal's employee, Mr Ferri of impeccable manners, had been thorough. Everything was restored to my possession. Yet again I was fitted out in the clothing of a gentleman of the Papal Court. I put on the black habit, the long justacorps and short breeches, as well as fine silk stockings over my shoes. With my cloak, powdered wig and tricorn hat I looked like an Ambassador of Cork Corporation sent to the Ascendancy Parliament of Dublin in the last century. I was ready for the flight northwards to Livorno, 'floundering / In the lamplight of quays' as the incomparable Oscharchigi has written. My wanderings in Rome were not over, for the two men took me across the ill-lit city yet again, Mr Barry all the while discussing the merits of Titian, his chiaroscuro and colouring, his *Venus Rising from the Sea*, his *Portrait of Castiglione*, his *Allegory of Human Life*, the shadowy traffic of the night giving us three creatures a wide berth. Two constables detained us near a rowdy tavern while Mr Barry pronounced upon the lack of grace and beauty of the painted mistress of Philip II, but at the mention of the name of Cardinal Rezzonico they bowed and withdrew. I could feel the cold sweat of fear on the back of my neck.

IX

WE SOON CAME to a building that I recognized. Like the wandering, passive officers of Il Capitano Oscharchigi's poetry, frozen upon that moment of beginning and of ending things, I allowed myself to be led through the exquisite corridors once more. Camilla received us and kissed my two companions before embracing me with genuine love and need for several minutes. I was hurried to a chamber by a man-servant who carried my belongings, now smelling, I thought, of the midden heaps of the nocturnal street corners of Rome. I removed my hat and cloak and shoes, and made full use of the bowl of tepid water and soap-stone that was left for me. When I re-emerged from my chamber the men were gone, but Camilla awaited me and began to talk. Her husband was away. She had waited for this day, she said, the day she would flee with me back to my *ultra-montane* islands. She kissed me and willed me to return her kisses. I did so, but not with kisses that were connected to my soul, for I was wise enough even then to understand that while I had lost my vocation I had not gained the new grace that is called a state of marriage. I tried to explain to her, with great sincerity and feeling, that I could never be a suitable companion to such a worldly and mature woman—for my own soul was hardly formed yet to meet the unsacramental world.

It is difficult to explain the atmosphere of that evening. In the stagnant and deeply ordinary life of an elderly man, such as I am now, it is not easy to recover those painful and beautiful complications of the heart that a youth feels; a Roman life of sentiment as distant now as the obelisk in the Campus Martius. We slept together that night, of course, for I was a Corkman and she was a passionate woman. But I remember nothing of the flesh. Dreams of that night I recall vividly, for I dreamt of the antique lion on the staircase of the Barbarini palace as described by Mr Barry as well as the oblique movement of the shielded Epaminondas at the Battle of Leuctra. I dreamt of poor Mr Barry too and his conversations on light; the difficulty of capturing it as it falls upon bodies, especially from great distances. Memory is like that too, I think, like the light that glimmers in a distance that cannot be delineated by any human eye. The poems of Il Capitano Oscharchigi did glimmer back toward us, us miserable creatures of unfaithfulness, still upon the point of embarkation, of flight from Rome:

> *And I still wandering,*
> *A vagrant in the mire of Piccadelio,*
> *Among people without Dukedoms*
> *And no trade to follow.*
> *Points of embarkation*
> *Will always be for me*
> *Like the Holy Bible's potter's field,*
> *A halting-site for Judas,*
> *A cemetery of the unsung.*
> *I await the awaited*
> *At nightfall,*
> *Attending, attending, attending.*

I woke constantly in the night, listening to Camilla breathing, never savouring the joy of lying a-bed with such a perfect Italian creature. The words of Oscharchigi come to my mind now as I remember:

> *Points of embarkation*
> *Will always be for me*
> *Like the Holy Bible's potter's field,*
> *A halting-site for Judas...*

We rose early and made our furtive and dishonourable departure. I pleaded with Camilla once more not to risk the long journey, not to place her marriage upon the path of ruin, not to dishonour her noble family name. But Mrs Furnari had made her preparations. Her packed cases and iron-rimmed trunks were placed upon a modest chaise; a coachman and postilion settled themselves on high and we were soon away on the road northwards through Terni. Fugitives from society, we had eschewed the road between Radicofani and Montefiascone and made tedious and disagreeable headway along the edge of steep precipices, many times having to dismount and persuade our coach and horses over steep, boulder-strewn roads. At Civita Castellana we lodged at a simple inn, throwing ourselves upon a meagre plate of eggs, wine and anchovies before retiring to a place of deep slumber. We moved on past Spoleto and headed on the road to Foligno, a beautiful valley of husbanded enclosures of cattle and corn, vines and olives. Onward to Perugia, the capital of Umbria, where we stayed a day, for Camilla wished to inspect the churches that housed pictures of Guido and Raffael, a tryst with memory, for she had last seen those pictures years before as a girl accompanying her father on business. At Perugia too we had the pleasant surprise of meeting Rev. John Hobhouse, Rev. Dr Charles

Dalkieth and the Admiralty forger, now attired as a priest, who remained with us for days until we reached the ferry point on the river Arno beyond Ancisa. They were the most agreeable companions and their company animated the humour of Camilla who in society and experience was more their kindred spirit than I. We parted from them at the ferry-boat for they wished to push on in the early evening, aiming to reach Florence by one of the two night-gates that are kept open for the accommodation of travellers. Camilla did not wish to submit herself to the extra scrutiny and more thorough examination of personal belongings that are the lot of strangers who enter Florence after sundown. We remained an extra night on the far shore of the brown Arno.

We did not dwell at Florence, but headed onward to Lucca, this strange direction in our journey because Camilla had friends there who would not subject her to frightening censure for having left her husband. For days they had awaited us upon the great south rampart of Lucca, coming every day at noon, they said, to await Camilla's arrival. They had prepared lodgings for us, as well as victuals and stabling for the coach and crew. It was here at Lucca, in the home of Camilla's friends, that I came into contact with Il Capitano Giancarlo Oscharchigi. The city of Lucca, therefore, remains in my soul as a place of benediction, a place of gifts. The Captain-Poet had accompanied a group of Jewish diamond merchants from Conegliano Veneto, protecting his charges with a lively company of Veronese dragoons. The party had come to Lucca for happy personal reasons as well as business. A kettubah, or illuminated marriage contract, had been especially commissioned from a skilled calligrapher at Lucca and it was Il Capitano Oscharchigi's happy duty upon his return to the Veneto to deliver this contract into the hands of a bride's wealthy family. Buoyed up by the happiness of the moment, good trade in diamonds and the promise of an atmosphere of love, the Captain-Poet presented me with one of his collections of poetry, a perfectly printed book of Torino, now a rare bibliographer's prize in the world of Italian poetry. We talked for more than three hours on that evening, touching upon the awesome, patriotic duties of the soldier and the conflicting but necessary self-absorption of the poet. He spoke about the difficulties of war in the Austrian provinces and the beauty of the foothills of Cortina. I told him about the unhappy kingdom of Ireland, the unfair subjugation of the common people and this made him very angry; an unnecessary anger that filled me with a deep sense of brotherhood towards him and the people of Italy who always hold nothing but the deepest sympathy and pity for the Irish. It is one of the great fortunes of my life to have broken unleavened bread with one of Italy's greatest poets, a good fortune that I never grow tired of telling my children. I am certain that they are weary of my tales of Italy, but indulge their doting father with a tolerance and kindness they inherit from their mother.

From Lucca, Camilla and I moved on to the coast, making slow progress through a rain-soaked countryside. Friends in Ireland can never quite believe my reports of the heavy April rains of north-western Italy. Camilla, certainly, grew impatient, an impatience bordering on panic, with the deep ruts and quagmires of mud that halted our coach, and forced the coachman to dismount, remove our luggage and assist our horses with the effort of pulling. I wonder if it was the stress of that last journey, the strain of never knowing what terrain awaited us as we journeyed, sometimes in darkness, through the countryside, that created an aura of separateness between Camilla and myself by the time we reached Livorno. We arrived at the sea, at this only port of the Duchy of Tuscany, in an atmosphere of separateness. Perhaps Mrs Furnari was having second thoughts as the prospect of a sea journey to Marseilles opened up before us. And after Marseilles, the long coach journey through a rain-soaked France until we reached Bordeaux and a Hennessy ship that would take us home to Ireland.

Livorno was then a handsome and well-built city of two havens, one for the Duke's guns and one for the merchant fleet, defended by twelve forts and a mighty rampart with its garrison of two thousand men. We lodged at a luxurious inn for four nights, venturing abroad as freely as husband and wife to inspect the fine coral manufactory and the even finer canal that links this port city to Pisa. Here was a great Jewish trade, an energetic and cultured population of the sacred yarmulkah that carried on the English triangular trade of coral, silver and diamonds whilst the Duchy itself was content with its monopoly of salt, tobacco and brandy. While promenading on the streets and dining in the coffee-houses we heard many stories of the sea, of the depredations of the Barbary corsairs, of the frigates of the Order of Malta that protected ships in convoys of the Maltese-Barcelona cotton trade. One *vascello* of the Maltese fleet had been destroyed by a corsair in recent months, and this intelligence filled Camilla with added trepidation.

Finally, on the morning that I booked passage on a merchant ship sailing for Genova and Marseilles, Camilla did reveal her deepest fears and decisions. She wished to return to Lucca, to her friends who might become an Embassy on her behalf to her husband in Rome. I was saddened, but not surprised, by her announcement for I had anticipated some kind of resolution to the estrangement that was growing between us as a result of our exhausting flight. I was too young then for the wax of eternal fidelity to harden. Camilla said that Mr Barry might help her, for he too had left Rome and was travelling north with her sister. They might meet her in Lucca or Florence. I wondered how she had come into possession of this knowledge, for we had received no correspondence, nor met any familiar persons in all the time we spent upon the streets of Livorno. I thought with envy of the companionship to be found at Lucca, of the many kind faces and the prospect of meeting Il Capitano Oscharchigi and continuing the profound conversations of the dinner table. I would be left upon these quays, I thought, like 'a mere mascot hound, / Craning my neck for salvation, / Hound without knowledge, / A mere dog of the Regiment'.

We returned to our chambers after she had made her clear preferences known to me. Decisiveness, I thought, became her, for she did not flinch or weep while announcing her future to me. It was as if love was a matter of business, a kind of disinterested transaction. It was only when we had lain together that the flood-gates of longing were flung open, and she wept for the wickedness of what she, a married woman, had done to me. But I did console her. I did entreat her to accept that I was an adult, a man of no experience, but an adult nonetheless, and one in full possession of his faculties. I could not blame alcohol, for example, or any of the fine brandies imported by the Duke, for my own loss of discipline. In matters of adultery two adults, not one, must always share the sour fruit of damnation before God in Heaven. She clung to me for forgiveness' sake, and locked in that desperate embrace of lovers who fail, we fell into a deep sleep.

When I awoke she was no longer by my side. Everything that she possessed was gone, every jewel and piece of clothing, every trunk and *escritoire* and vase. She could not have fled without the aid of servants; of servants whom she must have engaged without my knowing. It has ever been a mark of my character that I am not observant of the ordinary and domestic realities of life; a lack of attention to general things that has often given my wife Louise much amusement and a little annoyance. My Louise has always said that I have had an eye only for the foreign or bizarre aspects of the daily hour. This lack in observational powers has kept me safe from danger throughout my life, for I know I have come through dangers that would have filled a more observant merchant with horror. In my life I have ever marched forward, unaware of the danger that lurks in the wainscoting or barely attached chimney-pot. And so it was during the last hours of my last day in Italy. When I rose from my bed with a desolate and truly abandoned heart I moved automatically and unconsciously, like one of my wife's cats that has stumbled upon the form of some unexpected little prey in the distant grass. Upon my table was a man's vest, a frail garment that Camilla must have purchased from the Hebrew company of Conegliano Veneto; and resting upon the garment was a note in her hand, a farewell message and an admonition to get to the merchant haven early in the afternoon so that the boat for Marseilles would not have sailed without me. She must have thought me so idle and disorganized that I might forget my journey homeward. Appended to her farewell note were the names and London addresses of two persons, one a Mr Oppenheim and the other a Lord Hyde of Duke Street, St James.

It was not until I had reached Marseilles, and was safely lodged on the road to Bordeaux—thinking suddenly of Luke Cleary left in Rome, ever on retreat but bound for a distinguished priesthood—that, grown curious by what I thought were spare but hidden jasper buttons, I unthreaded the silk lining of this vest and discovered the patrimony of Italy and the worldly inheritance of my first love. Sewn into the lining of my new vest were seven diamonds, cut and polished beautifully in the manner of Antwerp or the general Dutch diamond trade. The gems glinted in my lap as I dislodged them one by one at the window of a humble French inn. In size they were out of the ordinary, and I knew at once that I possessed a sudden prodigious wealth. I knelt instantly upon the bare floor by my bedside and prayed to God in thanksgiving, for I knew I had been blessed by God and forgiven by Heaven in the form of Camilla Furnari. I have ever been blessed by Heaven since childhood, and I thought in my priestly innocence that God had once more visited me with a Heavenly forgiveness for my wickedness. Through Camilla's diamonds I would become the rescuer of my father and the Murphy business at Cork.

When I reached Ireland after several weeks I did not go directly to Cork, but arranged to journey to London to speak with Mr Oppenheim and Lord Hyde. It was through Mr Oppenheim that I gained entry into the society of Lord Hyde, a second son of the Earl of Jersey, who, with the Oppenheims acting as my honest agent, purchased outright the seven diamonds that were later part of a Royal wedding gift. When I reached Cork again, in late May of 1771, I possessed a fortune of eleven thousand guineas. Upon learning of this fortune, my father instantly forgot my lost vocation and fretted instead upon the source and true ownership of my money. For ten years after my return he expected at every moment of the day that constables of Cork Corporation would arrive to arrest me at our offices, but no constables ever came. I felt as rich and honoured as Thomas Pitt, Governor of Fort St George, who fifty years earlier had sold his great diamond to the Duc d'Orléans.

In truth a tremendous drain was placed upon my fortune in the early years, for contracts, cargoes and employments seemed to lose the family money at every turn. By the mid-1780s more than three-quarters of my reserves had ebbed away. My mother fretted greatly for my sake, and did wisely persuade me at that time to place two thousand guineas in secure bond at London where the exigencies of the ocean trade would not destroy my holdings. At that time the financial affairs of Irish Catholics were everywhere complicated by laws and scrutinies, so that I am ever grateful to the late fathers of Mr Isaac Hewitt and Mr J. W. Newsom for becoming my nominees. My children, also, shall honour their good Protestant names with favour and kindness.

Much water has flowed under the wooden bridges of Cork and many cargoes have been delivered or lost upon the sea since I first returned to Ireland with these sacred texts of Italy's greatest poets. For me Italian poetry is a matter of friendship and memory, not one of scholarship or academic advocacy. In the early years after my return to Cork the poems of Il Capitano Giancarlo Oscharchigi helped me to maintain my spiritual and personal equilibrium. Without Oscharchigi I should have floundered, and left Cork, perhaps, to try a different life in the Americas. But it was the contemplation of Italian intellectual life that made Cork bearable for me before I discovered the universal solace of wife and family, the common refuge of decent men in Cork as elsewhere.

Count Luigi da Pora, Monsignor Limnio di Murthillo, Principessa Nulana Nigonelli and Il Capitano Oscharchigi: these, then, are the four poets whose voices still remain with me from that distant Roman sojourn of my youth. Although they existed and composed exquisite verse in a land of Duchies and Kingdoms that is now collapsed, a land that may never be recovered by us again, they remain as sublime companions of my private soul. Their work—a product of the middle and higher echelons of Italian society—has been borne happily by me from youth to sanguine old age. The tenderness of Giancarlo Oscharchigi, the forceful exactness of Count da Pora, the disconsolate bravery of Principessa Nigonelli and the faithful solemnity of Monsignor di Murthillo, all have deepened my life and remained as an heroic ornament in days of personal darkness. When Louise

146

and I did lose our first-born child in the early years of our marriage, it was to the Principessa's work we turned in our most private grief, to find therein a solace of motherhood and a maternal stoicism. The work of Monsignor di Murthillo has endured for me as an heroic ornament in a world darkened: it was to his poems I turned in the weeks following the loss of two uninsured Caribbean cargoes to privateers on the second leg of their split voyages (how I cursed and railed against the rivalries in Trade of the Great Powers, how I admired the armed and purposeful neutrality of Denmark and Russia). In the months following dear Bishop Bernstein's death in a logging tragedy on the banks of the Mississippi in the Americas, it was to Count da Pora's great work I turned, and found therein a strength of character and life-affirming vivacity. Bishop Bernstein would have loved such work had I translated it for him before he departed the shores of Europe.

These poets of Italy mean something entirely personal to me. When I speak aloud their beautiful un-Irish names, startling the clerks who work at our offices in Penrose Quay, I am transported back to a time when I was young and foolish, but not entirely innocent. I recall the intensity with which Mr Barry recited these works of Count Luigi da Pora, and I hear the poems of Il Capitano Oscharchigi recited in the Roman accent of Mrs Furnari, that great love of my own youth. For many years I have recited these poems to my wife, Louise, who would never wish that the story of these texts should be suppressed. Men who deny the foolishness of their youthful loves in a completely misguided effort to hide their early liaisons from the true companions of their maturity—such men are completely untrustworthy in the deep universe of human feeling. They are but half-companions in the final romance of a long marriage.

X

WE LIVE IN important times. In Cork the artistic world has flourished anew. This year Mr Bolster will publish his miscellany *Harmonica* with sublime poems from authors as young as eighteen years. I must admit to having six of my own original compositions published therein as well. Recently we had a most powerful reading from Mr Matthew Hartstonge Weld's *Minstrelsy of Erin*, published to great acclaim at Edinburgh, and Rev. Zachariah Worrell gave a tremendous rendering of his *Poems on Moral and Religious Subjects* to an enthusiastic Cork audience last November. Later this year, Sydney Lady Morgan is expected at Cork to speak of her forthcoming work, *Verses to Marianne Howard*. We live in an atmosphere of heightened expectation, therefore, and this feeling that a new year may bring us brilliant and unexpected new voices in literature keeps us young at heart. In London, our own Tom Moore has become a poet of national fame, fêted in the company of Dukes and Generals. My hopes for these poets of Italy are more modest: an edition of seven hundred copies, with a supplement to follow containing the full texts. I have already pre-sold two hundred copies to Mr Atkinson for the Boston book trade. Mr Atkinson, a distant cousin of Mr John Lockhart of Edinburgh, says that Boston may yet be the salvation of the book trade of these kingdoms. With such a modest print-run we will never face the censure reserved for conspicuously famous persons, such as the author of *English Bards and Scotch Reviewers* did trenchantly pass judgement upon:

> *'No! when the sons of song descend to trade,*
> *Their bays are sear, their former laurels fade.*
> *Let such forgo the poet's sacred name*
> *Who rack their brains for lucre, not for fame.'*

Although no bank-draft of one thousand guineas will be waged upon this Cork Marmion, or forty thousand copies see the light of day, we intend to courier a modest quiver of this memoir to our sister city, Edinburgh, the Athens of the North: the true voice of poetry reaches everywhere without too much prompting. Like dear Mr Barry, I believe that true art has built within it an undeclared rendezvous with fame. To hear Count da Pora's words in Italian, to hear the voice of the Principessa Nigonelli, is to be tumbled by the deepest fame. It is part of the genius of poetry that its effect can be captured and translated. I hope the supplement of my full texts planned by Mr Harris for next Christmas will prove this point. Mr Bolster, our most distinguished Cork personage, is of the opinion, also, that the poem is hard and unassailable as a diamond and may be transported across languages with its essential value undiminished.

It may amuse persons who know me only as a merchant, and one who drives a hard bargain, to find a literary person hidden within the mass of Murphy Shipping accounts and manifests. For the last four years I have harangued a number of close friends at the Cork Library with these versions of Italian poetry. I am especially grateful to Mr J. N. Wrixon, Mr W. E. Penrose and Mr Bartholomew Gibbings, who all have encouraged me to publish this work; and who have subscribed monies to publish a luxury calf-bound edition in the manner of the earliest Italian edition of the Principessa Nulana Nigonelli. While I have the resources to print a modest book, I could not justify excessive expense to my children and business partners. There is often a misunderstanding among those who are otherwise educated about the nature of business capital: a businessman is not at liberty to distribute or indulge capital upon a personal whim—a man is free only to use what has been declared in dividend at the close of a year's trading. Thus, while a merchant might appear rich in burdens of property, his banker would know a more accurate and sorry truth. I am grateful, therefore, for the resourcefulness of my friends. We have been indulgent *dilettanti* of translation, but faithful to the task at hand.

In conclusion, something of the pure genius of Italy can be seen at once in this 'Sonnet' of my Captain of the Venetian regiments. There are not many poems in any tongue as lyrical and beautiful as this work of Il Capitano Giancarlo Oscharchigi. Certain lyrics of Walter Scott and our own Tom Moore do approach in lyricism this love poem, but none contain that profound music of an Adriatic affection recaptured:

SONNET

In memory's album I preserve you,
Beloved boy, beloved, beloved.
Head of curls, eyes direct, beautiful you made
May for me. Divine image, O divine memory
In the labyrinth of deep thought.
That is what is made from you, ragazzo
Of May, unimpeachable boy.

In memory's album I preserve you,
Beloved boy, preserve you, preserve you:
May, those divine limbs of a boy,
As in secret I unlock your mystery
And trace you moistly in poems—
Head of curls, startled eyes,
Meltwater in the foothills of Cortina.

The subject of the poem was that dead youth of Mestre, a beauty fallen in its earliest bloom. In memory's labyrinth this beloved youth, this 'unimpeachable boy', is recovered after the lonely and circuitous journey of the Captain-Poet. Yet the journey taken, the form recovered, lies but in 'memory's album' where nothing can again be made to breathe with the love of living men. Love, the poet tells us, is as impermanent as the winter snows that pack the hills of Cortina. Memory itself is the uncovered road, where love is merely recaptured as a remnant. The poet returning falls fully upon a relique rather than a body. Ultimately, the youth who is desired can be loved only as an embodiment in verse. This is the tragedy of those who both desire another and wish to make art: poetry exists at that untenable place where time is delivered as a hostage. There is no art that does not contain grief at our being mere creatures of God's creation, mere instruments of Heaven. Christ's promise never quite reaches the poet's ear. Each poet fumbles through the labyrinth of a life, never knowing fully, as ordinary mortals do, that at the centre of this labyrinth is our own personal death. Stating this observation has made our Lord Byron suddenly famous, yet each of my Italian poets knew and accepted this truth fifty years ago. Our Europe of pure reason has lived only recently with the shadow of the guillotine, yet Italian poets have lived with the Judgement of Heaven for centuries.

When I have closed the book upon my Italian poets, as I have done nightly for these past four or five decades, I think of the great good fortune I had in early youth. Not many men are born with the advantages I stumbled upon while still very young. I think of the genius of Mr Barry, the unsettling kindness of Mrs Furnari, the friendship of Luke Cleary. In recent days I have been poring over the two volumes of Mr Barry's lectures and letters, published nearly ten years ago by Cadell and Davies in the Strand. Within those pages one can find also the many kindnesses that were bestowed upon James Barry by Mr Edmund Burke and his family. One can see the agitations and stresses of that brilliant mind. There is one letter of Edmund Burke, of September, 1769, that I wish to quote. No Irishman ever so loved the world of Trade and Beauty, of Mercury and Minerva, as Mr Burke. No man ever lived who loved British life as he did, yet understood the uncomfortable distinctiveness of Ireland and her need to control her own destiny. Here is this letter of Burke, written in reply to Mr Barry who had wished to undermine the charges of his enemies:

If you have improved these unfortunate quarrels to your advancement in your Art, you have turned a very disagreeable circumstance to a very capital advantage. However you may have succeeded in this uncommon attempt, permit me to suggest to you, with that friendly liberty which you have always had the goodness to bear from me, that you cannot possibly have always the same success, either with regard to your fortune or your reputation. Depend upon it, that you will find the same competitions, the same jealousies, the same arts and cabals, the emulations of interest and fame, and the same agitations and passions here, that you have experienced in Italy; and if they have the same effect on your temper, they will have just the same effects on your interest; and be your merit what it will, you will never be employed to paint a picture. It will be the same at London as at Rome; and the same in Paris as in London: for the world is pretty nearly alike in all its parts ... for nothing can be so unworthy of a well composed soul, as to pass away life in bickerings and litigations, in snarling and scuffling with every one about us. Again and again, dear Barry, we must be at peace with our species; if not for their sakes, yet very much for our own.

The other day, as I read of the wreck of a French frigate at Martinique, all souls on board perished, I watched our own charter, the *Bernard* out of Bristol, turn upon the road at Roche's Point. I thought how the seas, and ships upon the sea, connect us to each other in mortal interdependence. Poetry, also, is a kind of ocean upon which we trade abundantly. As a merchant in the port of Cork, I commend the trade of poems, that earthly commerce of the soul, to all who read these poets out of Italy. And I advertise the great Christmas supplement of texts that will follow before the year 1818 closes.

NATHANIEL MURPHY

Trade

Nathaniel Murphy Disembarks at Passage, 1801

Two days of storm in the channel, and now
    The calm:
This morning Cork Harbour sat upright after rain.
Our vessel, still majestic, with one torn sail,
    Rose with the spring-tide.

Spars and brass are freshened by showers.
I thought of my beloved son and daughters,
    My devout wife,
How we have gained passage through the century:

    How we had planned
And saved and traded and sought position—
Only to return to this storm-washed city,
    Its red speckled whisper of stone,
Its keen wind that cries of orphaned children.

How little of grief attends the harbour now.
    The last century
Becomes cured in the brine of so much trade.
    Through the blind eyes of trade
We miss the dead floating by on slaughtered spars.
    The life that attends to us
        Is well-clothed as a Rushbrooke chandler's agent.

He Considers His New Eye-Glasses, 1800

The Nineteenth Century now seems a smaller place
Since I hung these new eye-glasses on my face.
I stumble through congested Ship Street
With laughing Noblett Johnson and Isaac Hewitt

And remark how much smaller my own ship's become.
Even coopers at work seem to have more elbow-room.
Mr Hewitt, taunting me, says I should sue old Penrose
For what must now seem a narrower quayside lease.

But I reply, hanging like a spy-glass on my words,
That a smaller ocean is what I have worked towards
All my life. Safely harboured, the world shall come
To all of us. The new century narrows to face the storm.

He Recalls the *Jeanie*, America-Bound, 1775

Home but a month from the haven of Europe,
I stand with my father and watch John Kirkwood,

The *Jeanie*'s formidable Master,
Certify the weight of candles out of Cork.

We marvel at Messrs. Mure and Atkinson's
Merchant prestige, prestige well-earned—

Thirty-three thousand pounds of candles
For the use of His Majesty's forces:

Such a cargo of light, sent duty-free.
She sails on tomorrow's tide, the morning breeze—

So much light, my father said,
The sea-road will be lit from Cork to the Colonies.

At the Ordination of Father Layton, 1803

It is good to see the new trade in spiritual things
At times like these, the Kingdom at ease.
Yesterday, a new splendour of voices;
Such choral strength never seen in Cork;
A young priest turned to us with the arrogance
          Of a merchant.

Mr Layton's boy, it was, Layton of the fine
Hams and the spiced red beef.
Like his merchant father, the boy-priest
Has opened his own stall. In the strange bazaar
Of the new century he shall offer
The frail craft of his holy person, his neat beard;
          His one good Roman collar.

He Considers Four Young Nuns, 1789

I have risked my own license to trade
Out of our safe harbour for ships
By ferrying these persons from Havre—
Four confident young of the Sisterhood;
Friends of Joseph Nagle's niece,
Keepers of a long Blackrock lease.

Incautious in their Popery,
From Cove to Cove Street
They prattle with enthusiasm
In a language that terrifies
The purveyors of offal
In the new covered Market.

I caution them in a mild manner,
And they, embarrassed, enriched by exile
In the Rue St Jacques,
Take risks that would frighten a Bishop.
I admire their elegant manners,
So much boldness in a time of fear.

Ladies pass by in their sedan chairs,
But these daughters of St Angela Merici
Hold their simple skirts above the mud.
Imprudent in their Paris Latin,
They've not had to mind their manners.

Something of Havre has entered their blood.

He Considers Bishop John Bernstein, 1789

Great commotion upon the quay at Passage West;
A festive air as Bishop Bernstein is piped aboard.
From the corner College in Chapel Street
To the slated Mass-House in the South,
The Bishop takes his sumptuous leave.
Doctor McCarthy, co-adjutors and canons,
Cry all the way from Rabagh's Lane.
Bernstein has spurned an offer from Turnerelli—
'Boston, not bust,' he says. 'Let a Catholic sit instead:
I can't wait here for foreigners to copy my head.'

Society gasps at Bernstein's resolve—
To leave Europe's violin-enchanted quays
For a Bishopric in a sun-baked prairie.
Sunday last, before final Worship,
His Grace presented his new wife to the flock,
Cynthia, beautiful love-child of the St Patrick's Dean,
Who embarks with him on the stellar journey.

Bishop Bernstein sails upon the high tide,
The lovely Cynthia Swift by his side—
No more will Cork benefit through his erudite heart,
Nor Europe be blessed by such a feeling for Art.
The prairies, though, and all trading posts afar,
Will grow wise by his journeys. Over here,
We shall make do with epistles once a year,
A new dullness in learning, mere Italian casts.

He Meets Eight Presbyterians
Upon the Quays, 1829

My son vies with Isaac Solomon
For seven heavy plates of Ulster silver—
To no avail, for Isaac crowns his offer
With a cache of sea-faring pills
And an anti-cholera device that fumigates
With a magic vapour
Every Belfast trunk wanted on the voyage.

Neat in everything, courteous in grief,
This little band of Antrim farmers
Await the tidal goodbye, the sailing ship
That will take them to a Delta port.
Nothing of Cork has touched them,
Neither Peacock penury, nor Hammond prostitute.
Unsure of their safety in this southern place,

They speak to no one except on business.
New Catholic church bells go carolling
Over our sixty thousand destitute.
Our squalid fever-hospitals rotate
Around their Presbyterian destinies:
America calls them. They flee from us.
Cholera will not have them, nor Catholic Cork.

He Addresses the Committee of Merchants, 1818

Success it is that makes the soul complacent,
And dulls the edge of hunger.
We who for so long established a standard
Of food, who sent Cork firkins overseas,
Lisbon and Buenos Aires, Boston and Cadiz,
Now see the first yellow pages of complaint.

Here is a description of one filthy creel,
Left to mould and fructify on a Tagus quay.
Here is a letter of complaint
From the Spanish Inspectorate of Weights.
Here is the rancid evidence of poor cooperage,
Complaints initialled, certificates refused.

How simple it is to take one's eyes off a world
Where the glitter of silver is dulled:
Merchants of the long supper table,
A chamber of fools;
While cities fell or were disabled
We spent months complaining of candle and coal.

He Dines at the Nile Street Coffee-House, 1800

Bustle of morning traffic on Nile St,
A horse up-ending a midden cart,
A fruit crier, a shirtless urchin
In the chill of an April morning:

I see Master Comyn carried in his sedan chair
By two apprentice sycophants;
He floats above the world of those who work
With the effortless air of a Cork lawyer.

At East Ferry, 1801

Today, a pleasant August picnic at East Ferry—
One of the Company's ships at anchor
Beyond the Calf at Roche's Point:
She awaits her pilot on the tide
In this, the calm summer of the new century.

A light breeze blows from the East,
But the harbour is at rest, the weather-glass
Still high. Alderman Casey flirts with my wife,
Yet again. One-legged, he is incorrigible—
If he had two legs no woman would be safe.

He is the Napoleon of Montenotte's love-life.
He catches my eye and hesitates—
Yet lunges again across the picnic blanket.

His silver plate is laden with so many love affairs;
His frame creaking, like the caravels of Spain
On the high seas, as he pursues a pilotage of lust.

He Remembers His First Meeting
with James Barry, 1769

A flask of Orvieto
In the Osteria della Sybilla:
We sat together at the table
That intense October.
How he loved to talk
Of Blackpool and Blarney Street,
Of clumsy frescoes in red
Over Mick Flanagan's pub;

Of his enemies in Cork
Who were named, one by one,
Sainthill and Murphy, Dean
And Bastable, Joshua Healy too,
Even the friars of Broad Lane—
My blameless Franciscans—
Who owed him the carriage
Still, he said, of pigment sent

To restore a Ligurian vestment.
More than altar wine
Passed my lips as I took to him;
His hunted, dark eyes,
His tongue a pink sponge
Of vinegar, his person crucified
By every artless thief
That ever drew breath in Cork.

I should have known, that
Very moment of unconsecrated
Wine, the troubled part

He would play in my decline.
Rage, rage. His expletive
Pigments bleached my heart:
Only troubled persons, bitter
Wines, adhere to perfect art.

At the Castel S. Angelo in His Youth, 1770

It was you, Mr Barry of the Blackpool pub,
With your stone-mason's awl
Who prised the cunning marble
From the Roman prison wall.

Neither the vaulted interior of Hadrian's villa
Nor the mean gardens of Sallust—
That overwhelming nymphaeum—
Seemed as melancholy or cavernous
As one small gash in ancient blockwork.

What a little thing we stole from Rome,
A small bas-relief.
I have it still
And it speaks of the Mother of God,
Vestal, miniature, Mary's medallion,

To admonish me, and you too,
Fr Prout, wayward Mahony,
To admonish us both—
Sic transit gloria mundi—
For our lost apprenticeships
In the one true Italian Church.

He Remembers Cholera and Pine Trees at Naples, 1772

Cholera that respects no traffic or human trade
Greeted us at the Roman approach to Naples;

Cholera that Mr Barry said was an ensign
Flown from the mast of every port—

A pestilence that reminded him of Passage West;
Cholera that churns every saturated harbour

And smells of unforgiveness. For me as a failed
Priest it was a desperate metaphor:

For desperate Mr Barry, a mere colour.
Plastered thus across Campania was my failed life.

Cholera, chipped and mixed by Mr Barry's palette knife,
Was a pallor that came into his painting

As indifferent to my pain as the pale yellow of pines.

At the Adelphi, Thinking of James Barry, 1788

Waiting to claim his laurel wreath
Is Pindar with his Chorus,
And there, nestling at the feet of Hercules,
Is our Blackpool's Hellenic Mr Barry;
More timid and seeming ill-at-ease
Than ever was great Timanthes.

I think of our youthful time in Rome,
Us savage Thracians, would-be priests,
Before the soul's Enlightenment
Of Roman ease. A pale breast
Out of pure Canova marble, mere outline
Of love, welcomed me but came to rest

In Mr Barry's experienced palms.
Art claims this advantage over lovers
The way natural manhood never could:
Mr Barry received his lyre
From Apollo, not from the simple Pope.
Lust was his affable College Rector.

Think of our first Faith and its music,
And then the second lyre, love.
Two sister Muses instructed us
In its profane use. My prayer book
And daily office, Benedictions,
All things profound, fell away

At the first aromatic Roman kiss.
Sisters Centurioni, keeper's daughters,
Your influence I plainly see
In this paradise at the Royal Society—
Difficult to imagine Barry at ease
Except of a Roman post-coital *triste*,

Difficult ever to see Mr Barry
As harmonious as these panels
On a wall: not enraged or overwrought
About Mr Reynolds and all the English—
Not a beast of Water Lane—
But stunned Timanthes, quiet as a Greek.

He Remembers the Val di Comino, 1770

Wandering so far south with pugnacious Mr Barry,
I come upon a pear tree as ragged as my heart.

What little I have done to earn such fruit,
So little for Italy or Franciscan Cork!

Spoilt from companionship with Art,
I have tasted too much of what is not the Church.

I cannot get her face out of my heart; her olive
Skin so like the eternal promise of painting,

Her body now like the fruit tree that leans over me.
This town of Alvito, painted vista of the Abruzzi,

Is hardly real enough to quench our thirst:
We rest and pray under the Mater Ecclesia of pears.

He Recalls James Barry R.A., 1812

Stuck with a lode of salvaged ore in Passage,
I do business with mad and angry old Mr Barry,
Schooner captain and purveyor of porter.

His wretched boat moves across the shoals
Like an ill-clad boy in a History Painting
By his mad and wayward son. None of us,

Let it be said, among the smug and educated,
Could have foreseen the heavenly fill of sail
Blown up at birth in a Blackpool back-lane.

Today I consider our own gifted time in Rome;
Three of us praising Cork in the Trastevere,
Singing of Cork like drunken blackguards.

Our English companions turned away.
We were young once, and could embarrass the rich.
Time's varnish is slow to dry over the wet

Letters of credit and a Vatican keeper's girl.
We fled the secret copyists of eternal Rome:
Any Corkman would go mad remembering it.

He Reconsiders Mr Barry's
Neglected Gifts, 1830

Happy to be a purchaser of London prints,
I fall into an afternoon stupor of pride
Before Mr Barry's grand Adelphi gifts.
Never was the British Nation more aggrandized
Than in this set of Hellenic Irish oils:
Orpheus in action on the desert slopes of Thrace,
The harvest figure of Sylvanus and Pan,
War trophies from Salamis and Marathon;

And, over all of these,
The lovely triumph of Commerce,
Trade personified in the Thames—

And Mercury, that hard-headed Corkman,
Keeping his gaze
Fixed upon the immortals
Like the Admiral's dart upon the sea
                                   At Roche's Point.

His Tragic Sense of Life, 1831

I look upon Mr Barry's ambitious *Benefits of Trade*
And think of all the business we let slip away.
We could have had such profits from the Carolinas
And Bermuda. We allowed Bristol such sway

Over cotton bulk and Atlantic traffic.
Dull purveyors of dead cattle, importers of fuel,
We lost all our gentlemen, our book trade, silverware,
The luxury manifests of the Thames and Liverpool.

In the world of Harbour Masters we've become
The commercial mad, not unlike mad Mr Barry
Of the Passage trade who confused God-given gifts
With his everyday self, and died all at sea

In the world of art. He couldn't be keeper of mystery
And a trades-man both. Instead, he died in the throes
Of exiled wretchedness and London enmities:
In this life, this art, *quis custodiet custodes ipsos?*

He is Painted by Mr Daniel Maclise, 1830

Such an agreeable artist I have never met.
Mr Maclise jokes through this life
As if the century's problems could be eased
By the pungent seal of varnish.

But why does he insert the feathers
Of a cockatoo into my formal portrait?
Our company ships sail, it is true,
Into lush and distant islands;

But I am only the keeper of manifests.
It is Mr Maclise who has a cockatoo
In his soul. The birds that trouble me
Are the birds of the Marsh, thieves

Of seed grain and merchant wheat.
More art has gone into the cockatoo
Than into my face. Overpriced daylight
Falls upon this Patrick Street *atelier*.

This day sinks upon my confidence.
I should have had a sculptor do my face,
A Mr Hogan or the solid Mr Foley,
Instead of this birdman of chatter and paint.

He Reads a Poem of Dr Hickey's from Lisbon, 1831

Yet another brochure is sent from overseas,
Another book of verse in vacuous praise
Of clouds and mountains, hills and streams.
My Thomist and scholastic heart falls ill upon
Yet another heaven of plovers and eglantines.
How can so much of paradise be at hand
For these demented souls: as if
Heaven were that easy or that sublime,
Or even nature be the true inheritance of reason.

I remember the terrible grief of rain
As it soaked my mantle on Bianconi's cart
While I waited for a Regiment
Of Foot to pass by at Clogheen;
And I recall the blistering sun
Of early August, Rome,
And how my feet became ulcerated
With heat. How I hated the sun
When I was young, and heat's acidic element:

How I longed to be the Pontiff on his throne
And not a thing of nature, an Irish student-priest.
When I strolled with angry Mr Barry then
Between the compliant columns of the Vatican
I thought how lovely was the solace of art:
The lovely manufactured ease of pianoforte
Or painting or clouds made of thread.
Cloud and stream of our native land
Flowed lovelier for me on a varnished stand.

It was Rev. Dill-Wallace who sent to me,
Once, a frame of black silk
Entwined, like the Huguenot graveyard
At Carey's Lane, with a latticework
Of gold threads and green silk.
It was the magic work of his cousin, Mrs Delaney—
No bleak convolvulus or muscat grape
Ever smelled as true
As that work of nature by Dill-Delaney made.

It grieves me that Dr Hickey has succumbed
To a cult of nature that is rampant now,
A kind of false honesty of leaves.
Whereas the greatest truth I ever saw
Was on a piece of cloth
My daughter sewed. Black and silver
And encased in silk were plain,
Ungerminated seeds of honesty. I thought,
As I held her human effort in cloth,
The seeds but not the silk must soon be lost.

He Buys a Copy of *Childe Harold*, 1814

A September morning in Bolster's, the sunlit
Windows, the autumnal stationery.
I marvel at Lord Byron's limitless journeys;
So much a voyager, so little a merchant.

At Mr O'Ferrell's New Villa, 1826

A pleasant journey on the new Bianconi
Out of sunny Cahir and Clonmel—
I had the landscape read to me
By Mr Sullivan, the Callan merchant
Just returned from a Ball in Dublin:
He sees our land in a bilingual fashion
So that each bird and leaf lives twice.

Ablaze with our own native land,
(Mr Sullivan's way of seeing Ireland),
We darken the Palladian doorway
Of Henrich and Eliza O'Ferrell.
Inside, a rapture of violas and daughters;
The world turned from hemp to Art
In three short decades. We have seen Cork

Prosper from merchantmen in the Lee,
Customs at Cove, Bond-houses on the Quay.
It is music that has come from trade
Like letters from a Franciscan cousin
In Rome. Mr O'Ferrell, master ship-wright,
Twin nephew of a Rector and a priest,
Has brought home a trunk of antiquities.

His wife fusses over a bust of Artemis,
Fiddling about with wax and cloth,
Trying to invent lustre in Italian chalk.
Only time shall teach her to trust the dust.

I halt before a massive print of Tivoli,
Steep waterfalls as in Mr Beale's wood
All garlanded with grape and myrtle leaf.

Far from Art all the O'Ferrells were born,
Yet how enriched their souls have become
For having made the longer journey.

He Hears Memory and Praise
of Bishop Clayton, 1797

In my father's boyhood no one deserved the praise
Of Cork more than kind and eloquent Bishop Clayton.
Gone from God in the rules of our Church,
Love of travel beyond the Alps made him Roman.
Groves of myrtle grew about his blessèd heart,
Rectors and their mystical fraternity
Moved lightly in the breath of his opinion.
Pictures by Carlo, castles in the air by Vitruvius—
Strictures handed down by the mercantile élite,
All came to embarrassing grief at Bishop Clayton's
Stricter door of Venetian glass and wood.
Fall sinners may, but not the erudite of
His reign. All sang Catches then, and spoke of Love.
Disdain ill becomes us now, us foreigners to mirth.

He Learns of the Death of J.J. Callanan, 1829

How terrible it is to die on foreign soil,
So far from home and the company of sisters.
A ship from Lisbon brings the news:
My wife's youngest cousin dead,
A Munster poet in a springtime of verse:

The maids of Inchidoney will cry now,
I have no doubt. As the exiled Byron
Brought forth the wails of subject Greece,
Grief-stricken Missolonghi,
So the comfortless winds of West Cork
Shall weep for ours, dead at Sintra.

J.J. never found the fame deserved by a Callanan:
Nothing *Bolster's Magazine* could do,
Nor even the promise of help from Dr Maginn's
Illustrious boy on *Fraser's*,
Nor Crofton Croker's late intervention—
The honours of Edinburgh were beyond him.

I walk with Mr Bolster down Castle Street
And he speaks of a book to rival Murray's poet.
He dreams a *Childe Harold* out of J.J.'s death.
I can see but several perfect letters
And a little quiver full of sharpened poems
That will hardly set our United Kingdom alight.

For our cousin's life was an unfinished work
With four or five anxious beginnings;
Teaching and priesthood and medical work;
Unlikeliest of all, a subaltern's uniform.
Both learned and capricious, Byron-like, still
He never swam the Lavant that awaited him.

He Contemplates the Autumn of 1814

Leaves stain the quayside with abrupt rust
And branches, hawsers of red and gold,
Bend with the strain of an outgoing tide.
So much of ships rushing away, the promise
Here, left in ledgers and letters of introduction.
Somewhere in the Carolinas,
Soft with the autumn of Atlantic trade,
Is Cork summer bedded in, unrepentant.

From here, these windows of a merchant house,
The dead calm spreads upon harbour traffic.
Perished with October, leaves follow the pilot boat
While I wait behind in the prodigious city
Of trade—pencilling, filing in the shadow,
The long shadow of inappropriate oaks.

He Witnesses Another Hanging, 1813

Today we witnessed the adroit hanging
Of Margaret O'Malley, thief and countrywoman.
Last year her half-brother was shot at Mardyke fields
For the swearing of illegal oaths—
But wretched Mrs O'Malley, at Gallows Green,
Mother of five young souls,
Would this day be wholly alive
Had she not fallen in love
With a cupboard of her master's Belgian linen—

Though it was not her corpse, borne aloft
By a wailing crowd of Buttevant cousins,
That my friend, Homan Jephson, remarked upon
As we rested in the Nile St coffee-house:
No, not that—
But the fact that Homan had, at last,
Won the valued civil contract
To supply four years of hardened scaffold wood.

While we spoke he wiped his untroubled brow
With a crimson kerchief of imported cloth.

He Meets Lt. Hennessy, Cork Militia, 1799

A little pamphlet printed by Harris of Castle Street
Is pressed upon my burdened arms.
I hear the anxious voice of its frightened donor,
Lt. Hennessy who hankers still after his good name.
Nearly a year has passed by since it was lost
In the seditious town-lands of Wexford.

                  How dangerous it is
To try to save one's skin
In a Dungarvan sloop with three fair women
(Especially while churches burn).

He may never recover that lost tunic of manhood
Any more than my small boy shall recover
The four silver buttons
Of his best shirt
Lost at the Skellig Night in Grand Parade.

History tries its wickedness upon the weak-willed
And even more upon the wearer of uniforms:
Nothing for young Hennessy, now, methinks,
But to trade in butter between Youghal and France.

He Looks Upon Another Dead Child, 1803

The O'Donnells say it was the Fahys
Who started the trouble—
The Fahys of Borrisokane say
That O'Donnells are not true dancing-masters,
But only journeymen, *gubán saor*,
Teachers of common jigs and Clare sets.

Beloved wife, I write to you from the Clonmel Assizes
And regret that I've seen another dead child.
Whoever cast the first burning taper
Must answer before God alone. I thought
Of Amadé and the grief of his quiet mother:
Tell his father I've found the text of a poem.

I might add that young Stephen, of the Fahys,
Was never consulted about the long dispute.
When the O'Donnell mob came in the night
They cared not for the neutrality of a boy.

His soul was burned to a potato, his headless
Torso in a water-barrel, perfect, untouched by fire.

He Witnesses a Military Execution, 1804

I think of the great griefs of all our Regiments,
The kneeling and the frightened of the enfilade
Who shall be nameless in each History painting.

A roguish young Private of Hompesoh's Dragoons
Faces the Mardyke at his final hour.
He says that more than his companions' volleys
He fears the desolation of Caribbean exile—

And in the manner of all the unconnected,
A poor common soldier, his wish is granted.

He Considers the Misfortunes of Dublin, 1793

Hardly out of my Roman cassock, feeling foreign,
Irritable yet with the loss of Italian sun,

I came upon this person at the hour of twelve—
A chandler by the name of Matthew Conor,

His face full battered in, his tunic undone.
Speechless at the west end of Aungier Street,

He had all the melancholy signs of death.
I made feeble effort to aid this battered Matthew

(Too troubled still by my bankrupt cousin James,
His humiliating surrender to the bankruptcy court).

I watched this dying provider of light,
Attended at his bedside in the lodging-house

Until death sat upon his distressed body
With the peremptory ease of a coroner's court.

Meanwhile, all manner of domestic intelligence is
    enthralled
That the city of Dublin waits upon the Earl of Moira.

He Comes Upon the Cork Militia, 1798

Gentlemen and grey men of little or no consequence:
All seem the same in a military uniform.
I spy my old trading friend, John Cuthbert,
And his cousin Montfort Reagan at ease

When the Cork-bound coach reaches Lismore—
Two greater scoundrels never sold a side of beef.
I have the receipt, still, of Reagan's undelivered meat.
Their embodiment, now, in scarlet beggars belief

Although war that burns a respected soul
May provide the quick thief with escape outright.
The two make light of the dead of Wexford town
And praise, with coinage, their own delivery from grief.

He Purchases a Street Ballad, 1789

Caught in a downpour on Castle Street
I shelter at Mr Harris's blue door
And listen to one wretched balladeer,
A Mr Toomey of Adrigole,
Who sings for his supper in wet shoes.
He sings from the depth of his Christian being

And convinces me to part in the rain
With two tainted Irish pennies.
Wretched and landless, singing in sleet,
He makes an historic statement of sorts,
Blaming History for his present grief
As if History had a hand in the taking of land,

Or the leaving of sheep in a bed of excrement.
Words tumble from his dispossessed mouth:
In Castle Street rain it is the poor man himself
Who is History. I take his ballad-sheet,
His one title-deed, a thing discovered already,
Now rained upon, now perishing in my hand.

He Walks the Marsh, 1824

A still night as I walk with Dr Patrick Callanan—
Cousin of the poet and my wife's dearest cousin.
We listen to the night cries of children in unlit lanes.
Dogs barking at the carriers of fever. There is no end

To the pestilence that crowds the Infirmary.
The poor crumble before our businesses;
They hustle at the best corners, they accumulate
Like the mottled skins of sucked oranges.

If they keep dying here it will be the end of trade.
How can we keep them to their places of birth?
The wild countryside throws its poor upon Cork
As if the city were an Ark on the salt marshes.

We are angry at the Absentees who sucked them dry;
Who stay away from the unfashionable places of fever
While we walk without courage through the lanes;
Moving by ear, beyond where lamplight penetrates.

He Loses a Silver Buckle, 1797

All the troubles of our troubled Kingdom,
Terrible seditions, illegal oaths:
The closing of my favourite chop-house
In Nile Street, the going-out of lamps.

All of this is brought home to me
On a rainswept Thursday night:
My foot flapped like the foot of a servant
Indentured for the boat at Cove.

In too great a haste to save good time,
I lost a silver buckle loved by me;
Searched the ill-lit streets, cursed the Lee;
My buckle press-ganged by the rising brine.

His Tattered Copy of *The Mineral Waters of Ireland*, 1794

I blame Doctor Rogers for the crowds at Mallow.
It was he who brought Rutty to the springs;
Fashionable Mallow as medicinal
As the unpleasant baths at Aix-la-Chapelle.

Catarrh, coughs and asthma,
Diabetes and the scour, unpleasantness of breath,
All found their way by Rutty's book
To the most fashionable Spa Glen.

There is medicine in mere travelling.
It is strangers who get excited
By what they observe; more cured,
I think, by travelling far away.

Yet tourism is the catarrh of good trade.
This Friday a grain cart was toppled
By drunken foreigners out of Dublin:
Gamblers whose lives were already unmade.

I blame *The Mineral Waters of Ireland*
And all who place our names in books.
Publishers, poets, foreigners with gout—
All conspire against the good of trade routes.

He Sees a Warehouse Burning, August, 1798

Drawn by smoke and spills of burning cloth,
I run to Isaac Hewett's Distillery house.
A sheet of flame illuminates the summer night,
The crackle of fires like torn tackle and sail,

The screams of labourers and water carriers
And bringers of scarlet buckets of sand
Pierce the quayside and the blaze:
The intoxicated blaze, that *fou incensé*,

Leaping from windows and reddened beams.
I see Isaac with an empty bucket in his grasp,
Isaac at the point of giving in, of running away,
Flanked by his eldest boy, Isaac George.

I place my hand on his dear Protestant head
And he turns to face me, worn and devastated.
Sparks shower above us like a new Liberty Tree.
Without speech, we share the grief of friends.

He is Overwhelmed by Edinburgh in Old Age, 1831

A joy it is to walk these hallowed streets,
Edinburgh of the great Baronet and Mr Jeffries:
So much in love with poets and trade,
I prayed to see Edinburgh before I die.

Last night I met, most briefly,
Mr John Lockhart. He did remember Cork.
He recalls that visit to the Groves of Blarney,
And the sudden fame of Maclise's portrait.

He remembers us, as the Scots know Ireland,
As a land that leaves a light impression
Like tracings sent to Edinburgh
For a lithograph of his famous in-law father.

I would that we could make a deeper cut
Upon the harder skin of these Northern lives;
We light-hearted traders in wheat and meat,
We Cork painters of the unimportant skies.

He Encounters the Poor of Cork Harbour, 1829

Hands outstretched in a prayer for alms,
They offer up a blessing on our work.
I pass quickly on
With Mr Isaac Hewitt and Mr Johnson.

Since our firkins were packed with salted butter
And stamped with the prosperous indigo
Of our native, teeming port
The poor of the world have flocked to Passage West.

There is no end to the unhappiness
Of elsewhere, Mr Hewitt says. The word is out
That we may have excess victuals to spare,
Our grain spotted by the circling birds of hunger.

Mr Hurley of Kanturk, Mr O'Ferrell of Cork,
Have seen the eyes of persons whose blood
We cannot know, the world's angry, prophetic eyes,
Fall upon firkins of Cork. *Dear God, fall upon us*

As the destitute fall into every troubled port.